The Children of Fatima

by
Mary Fabyan Windeatt

Illustrated by
Gedge
Harmon

Nihil obstat:

   Richard P. Grogan
   Censor deputatus

Imprimatur:

   ✠ *Joseph E. Ritter, D.D.*
   Archbishop of Indianapolis

Feast of the Immaculate Heart of Mary

August 22, 1945

TO

THE IMMACULATE HEART OF MARY

QUEEN OF THE MOST HOLY ROSARY

QUEEN OF PEACE

TO WHOM

THE CHILDREN OF FATIMA

WOULD HAVE DEDICATED

THIS BOOK

By the Same Author

SAINTS IN THE SKY
The Story of Saint Catherine of Siena

MY NAME IS THOMAS
The Story of Saint Thomas Aquinas

LAD OF LIMA
The Story of Blessed Martin de Porres

ANGEL OF THE ANDES
The Story of Saint Rose of Lima

HERO OF THE HILLS
The Story of Saint Benedict

WARRIOR IN WHITE
The Story of Blessed John Masias

LITTLE SISTER
The Story of Blessed Imelda

LITTLE QUEEN
The Story of Saint Therese of Lisieux

NORTHERN LIGHTS
The Story of Saint Hyacinth of Poland

SONG IN THE SOUTH
The Story of Saint Francis Solano

I WAS THE PARISH PRIEST OF ARS
The Story of Saint John Vianney

THE CHILDREN OF FATIMA first appeared in serial
form in the pages of THE ROSARY and THE GRAIL.

Contents

Chapter One
The Angel of Peace . . . . Page 1

Chapter Two
Another Visitor . . . . Page 9

Chapter Three
The Lady Comes Again . . . . Page 17

Chapter Four
The Message . . . . Page 25

Chapter Five
A New Life . . . . Page 33

Chapter Six
An Unexpected Journey . . . . Page 42

Chapter Seven
The Test . . . . Page 50

Chapter Eight
The Fourth Visit . . . . Page 58

Chapter Nine
New Crowds in the Cova . . . . Page 67

Chapter Ten
The Great Miracle . . . . Page 76

Chapter Eleven
The Victims . . . . Page 87

Chapter Twelve
The Bells Toll in Fatima . . . . Page 98

Chapter Thirteen
The Great Sacrifice . . . . Page 109

Chapter Fourteen
To Lisbon . . . . Page 119

Chapter Fifteen
Farewell to Fatima . . . . Page 130

The author is deeply grateful to the Reverend William A. Hinnebusch, O.P., Ph.D., and to the Reverend John C. Rubba, O.P., Litt.D., both of the Faculty of Providence College, Providence, Rhode Island, for their generous help and encouragement in preparing this story of the apparitions of Our Lady of the Rosary at Fatima.

Chapter 1 — The Angel of Peace

IT WAS a cool spring morning in the year 1916 in which the three children, natives of the Portuguese village of Fatima, saw nothing unusual. As was their custom, they had arisen before dawn, eaten breakfast, then driven their parents' sheep to pasture. There had been the usual chatter along the road, the usual plans for games once the sheep were dispersed. And now it was raining, the chill drizzle that was to be expected in early spring.

"We mustn't get too wet," said six-year-old Jacinta. "Lucia, maybe we should go to the cave today."

"Of course we should!" cried her eight-year-old brother Francisco. "It would be easy to watch the sheep from there."

Their cousin, aged nine, surveyed the dreary landscape with a critical eye. This pasture where they had brought

1

the sheep belonged to her parents. It was only a small field with a few straggling rows of olive trees at one end, but there was also a little rise of ground nearby, surmounted by a windmill. In the side of this hill was the cave—assuredly the best shelter the place afforded.

"All right," she said finally. "You carry the lunch boxes, Francisco, and see that they don't get wet. I guess the sheep will be all right by themselves for a while."

A bit breathless, the three finally reached the cave. It was dark inside, and rather cramped, but the young shepherds gave no thought to this. They were used to the place, for they frequently played here even on sunny days. Besides, the cave was dry and commanded a good view of the pasture. It would be easy to notice it if the sheep began to stray.

For a while the children amused themselves with talk. Was it going to rain all day? Or would the sun come out so that they could play the Echo Game outside on the hill?

"I do hope the sun comes out," said Jacinta, shivering a little. "It's going to be dull if we have to stay in this place all day."

Francisco agreed, although he was not too interested in the Echo Game. Of course it was fun to stand on the hill-top and shout different words into the still country air, then hear them come back from the distance. But it was even better to hunt through the pasture for stones, drag them into place and then build a house.

"If it clears up, I'll build a really *big* house," he told the two girls. "It'll be the finest house you ever saw!"

Lucia laughed. Francisco was a year younger than she. Since he was a boy, he was a little inclined to think himself skilled at house-building. Yet he knew, and Jacinta knew, that it was really Lucia who was the leader. And why not?

2

Wasn't she the oldest? And the only one of the three children who had made her First Communion?

"We can decide what we'll do later," she said. "Right now let's see what we have for lunch."

An hour later the children had finished the bread, fruit and cheese which their mothers had packed for them. Then, seeing that the rain was almost over, Francisco suggested that they go outside to play. But Lucia would not listen. It was noon, wasn't it? And they had finished their lunch? Very well. Now they must say the Rosary, as was the custom of countryfolk for miles around.

Francisco sighed. He had never been very fond of the Rosary—or of going to church. Deep in his heart was the feeling that such things were meant for women and girls. Yet there was no use arguing with Lucia, and so he fumbled in a pocket and brought out a small wooden rosary.

"Hurry up, then," he said, "and as soon as we finish, I'm going to build the stone house. Just wait until you see how big and beautiful it is!"

For a few minutes all was peaceful in the cave as the three children told their beads. But a passer-by would have been very much surprised at the manner in which the little shepherds honored the Mother of God. To save time, they said only the first two words of the *Our Father* on the large beads and the first two words of the *Hail Mary* on the small ones, for long ago they had discovered that in this way an entire Rosary could be recited in the twinkling of an eye!

Presently their prayers were finished, and Francisco looked hopefully at Lucia. "Now we can go and play?"

"No. It's still raining."

"But just a little!"

Jacinta gave a quick glance outside the cave. "It's only a fine mist, Lucia."

"That doesn't matter."

"But the house! I want to start looking for stones!"

"You stay with me, Francisco. You, too, Jacinta. We can have a game in here."

Reluctantly the two children sat down again on the dirt floor of the cave. Lucia was the oldest, and long ago they had been told that they must obey her whenever they spent the day away from home. But as they sat, amusing one another with stories, a sudden gust of wind caused them to look up. Before they could worry as to whether or not a fresh storm was brewing, an amazing sight greeted them. Above the straggling olive trees at the far end of the field was a beautiful white light. It shone like the purest snow, the clearest crystal! But it was not still. It was moving— across the tops of the trees, across the open expanse of pasture, towards the cave!

The three children stared in awed silence as the strange glow approached and they saw that in its very center stood a young man. He wore flowing white garments such as the three had noticed in pictures of angels and saints in the parish church. But this was no picture. It was real!

"Fear not," said the stranger, smiling at the frightened youngsters. "I am the Angel of Peace." Then, kneeling, he touched his forehead to the ground. "Pray with me," he said.

Scarcely knowing what they did, the little shepherds fell upon their knees and imitated the actions of the strange young man. When he spoke, they repeated his words:

"Oh, my God, I believe in Thee! I adore Thee! I hope in Thee, and I love Thee! I ask pardon for those who do not believe, do not adore, do not hope, and who do not love Thee."

4

Three times the angel said this prayer, then arose and smiled again upon the children. "Pray thus," he invited. "The Hearts of Jesus and Mary will hear your petitions."

The next moment he was gone, leaving the children more awestruck than they had ever been in their lives. Indeed, when they returned to their homes that night, they could not bring themselves to speak of the day's great event to anyone. Somehow the angel's visit was too holy and beautiful for words.

It was not until midsummer that the angel came again. "Pray! Pray a great deal," he told the children this time. "The Hearts of Jesus and Mary have merciful designs on you. Offer prayers and sacrifices continually to the Most High."

Lucia hesitated, wondering whether or not it was proper to speak to an angel. Then a wave of courage swept through her. "How are we to make sacrifices?" she asked.

The heavenly visitor smiled. "Make everything you do a sacrifice and offer it as an act of reparation for the sins by which God is offended and as a petition for the conversion of sinners. Bring peace to our country in this way."

Jacinta and Francisco were silent. *Our* country! What did the angel mean? He didn't live on earth but in heaven! And how could children convert sinners? Or end the terrible war that had been going on in Europe for two years?

The shining spirit seemed to read such thoughts. "I am the Guardian Angel of Portugal," he said. "Remember these words: *Accept and bear with submission the suffering sent you by the Lord.*"

With this he was gone, and suddenly the children found themselves with strangely heavy hearts. Why did the angel have to leave them? Why couldn't he tell them more about how to convert sinners and when the war was going to end?

"Maybe he'll come again," suggested Francisco hopefully.

"And give us another message," added Jacinta.

Lucia nodded. "I think he will come," she said slowly, "but first we must pray and make sacrifices as he told us."

The angel did come again in the fall of that same year, while the children were out in the fields with their sheep. But this time he bore a golden chalice in one hand and a Host in the other. Amazed, the youngsters noted that drops of blood were falling from the Host into the chalice and that presently the angel left both suspended in mid-air and prostrated himself on the ground. Then came the beautiful voice they had learned to love:

"Most Holy Trinity—Father, Son, and Holy Ghost— I adore You profoundly. I offer You the Most Precious Body, Blood, Soul and Divinity of Jesus Christ, present in all the tabernacles of the world, in reparation for the insults, sacrileges and indifference whereby He is offended. By the infinite merits of His Most Sacred Heart and of the Immaculate Heart of Mary, I beg of You the conversion of sinners."

The children joined in this sublime prayer to the Holy Trinity as best they could, but their amazement knew no bounds when presently the angel arose from the ground, took the Host in his hand, and beckoned to Lucia. He was going to give her Holy Communion as the priest did at Mass!

As they saw their cousin approach to receive the Host, the hearts of Francisco and Jacinta filled with longing. How wonderful if they could have this great privilege, too! But of course this was impossible. They were not like Lucia, who had finished the course of studies for First Communicants. Why, they knew only a very little of the catechism!

Suddenly the angel looked at them over Lucia's bowed head. "Come," he said, and taking the chalice from mid-

THE HEARTS OF FRANCISCO AND JACINTA FILLED
WITH LONGING.

air, he indicated that they should approach and kneel before him also.

The little shepherds stared, then slowly got to their feet. Surely the angel didn't mean . . .

"Receive the Body and Blood of Jesus Christ," he told them. "Make reparation for the crimes of sinners and give consolation to your God."

Chapter 2 — Another Visitor

IN THE weeks that followed, the little shepherds often thought about the Angel of Peace and his message. As though by a miracle, the two prayers he had taught remained fresh in their memories, and they recited them very frequently—kneeling with their foreheads touching the ground, as the angel himself had done. But alas! Although they hoped and prayed, the heavenly visitor came no more. Day after day they took the sheep to pasture, said the Rosary as they had done on the day of the storm, looked carefully in the cave and throughout the field. There was never any trace of their friend.

"But we can remember what he told us," said Lucia comfortingly. "We'll pray and suffer every day, so that many sinners will be converted."

"That way the war will end sooner, too," added Jacinta.

Francisco was a little puzzled. How were they going to suffer? They weren't sick. Their families were poor, but there was always enough to eat. And their houses were comfortable.

"Don't you remember when I asked the angel about that?" cried Lucia. "He told us to turn everything we do into a sacrifice by offering it to God. And he also said that we were to be patient. Francisco, surely you haven't forgotten!"

The boy shook his head. "Of course not. But aren't these things too easy? How can they convert sinners and show God that we love Him?"

"Don't ask questions. The angel told us what to do, and we should obey him."

On May 13, 1917, slightly more than a year after the angel's first visit, the three children were pasturing their flocks as usual. They were in a large hollow known as the Cova da Iria, about a mile from their homes in Fatima. The place was stony, and there was not much grass or water for the sheep. But these things could not be helped, since what good grazing land there was belonged to people who did not want the children's flocks coming onto their property.

When the youngsters had eaten lunch and said the Rosary, they began to discuss plans for the afternoon. What games should they play today?

"There are some nice stones over there," said Francisco hopefully. "I could build a house . . . "

This time Lucia did not argue. It was a beautiful afternoon, with plenty of sunshine, and it had been many days since they had built a stone house.

"All right," she said. "Come on."

As they ran across the field, a sudden flash of lightning

10

cut through the air. Lucia stopped in amazement. *Lightning?* On a beautiful spring afternoon like this? Surely not! But the faces of Francisco and Jacinta clouded with disappointment as they stopped short in their tracks.

"Did you see that, Lucia? It means we're going to have rain!"

The ten-year-old girl glanced doubtfully at the sky. "Maybe it won't be a bad storm."

"You can't tell. And lightning is terribly dangerous up here in the hills. It could kill all of us in a second!"

Francisco nodded. "I think we ought to get the sheep together and go home," he said. "I'll blow my horn and they'll start running."

Even as the children headed for the center of the field, there came a second blinding flash. All three jumped from shock, then looked fearfully about. What if they were to be struck by the dreaded lightning? Then their glances fell upon a small holm-oak tree a few feet away. Attracted by a light in its topmost branches, they lifted their eyes. Wonder of wonders! The light was flowing from the lovely form of a lady! There she stood atop the little tree, her feet hidden in a shimmering cloud!

The little shepherds drew back in awe, although each felt that the lady was kind and good. How could it be otherwise? She was like the angel, but far more beautiful than he. She wore a long white dress, and the white mantle over her head and shoulders was edged in burnished gold. Her hands were joined before her breast, and from the right hand hung an exquisite rosary of white pearls with a golden cross. Yet the three children were afraid—afraid of the strange whiteness and golden glow before them—so bright that it hurt the eyes.

11

"Don't be frightened," said a gentle voice. "I won't hurt you."

Reassured, Lucia ventured a little closer to the tree. "Who are you?" she asked the lady. "Where did you come from? What do you want?"

The beautiful lady smiled. "I come from heaven. I want you children to come here at this hour on the thirteenth day of each month until October. Then I will tell you who I am."

By now Lucia's fear had vanished entirely. "You come from heaven! Shall I go there?"

"Yes. But you must say the Rosary, and say it properly."

"And Jacinta?"

"She will go, too."

"And Francisco?"

The lady looked at the nine-year-old boy before her, and there was a rather reproachful smile upon her lips. "Yes, but first he must say many Rosaries."

For a moment all was silent. Then the lady asked the children if they were willing to offer themselves to God and to bear all the sufferings He sent them? Would they pray very hard for the conversion of sinners?

"Oh, yes!" cried Lucia. "We will!"

Once again the lady smiled. "Then you will have much to suffer. But thanks be to God, He Himself will strengthen you."

Suddenly Lucia remembered that two little boys had died in the village recently. Since the lady came from heaven, she might be able to tell them whether or not their souls were with God. Rather hesitantly, she asked her.

"One of them is in heaven," replied the lady. "The other is still in purgatory." Then, having once more urged the

12

"YOU MUST SAY THE ROSARY, AND SAY IT PROPERLY."

19

children always to say the Rosary devoutly, the beautiful stranger turned toward the east. Before their astonished eyes her body began to glide from the top of the little tree into the brilliant sunshine flooding the pasture. The next moment there was only the sunshine.

Slowly the young shepherds came to their senses—sad and lonely, now that the lady was gone, but excited with the thought that she had promised to come again.

As they discussed the great wonder, Lucia was the first to realize that only she had talked to the lady. Francisco and Jacinta had been silent during the entire length of the apparition—ten minutes or so. Then another amazing discovery was made. Although Jacinta had heard the beautiful stranger speaking with Lucia, Francisco had heard nothing. He had only seen.

"Tell me what the lady said!" begged the boy. *"Please!"*

Lucia did as he asked, while Jacinta listened with shining eyes. What a wonderful day this was—even more glorious than those when the angel had visited them. But suddenly the little one uttered a cry of alarm.

"The sheep, Lucia! They've strayed away!"

It was true. The sheep had wandered into a neighbor's field and were damaging the crops there. Fearing that they would be punished, the children ran quickly to drive the flocks from the forbidden pasture. A moment later, Lucia faced her cousins anxiously.

"We'd better not tell anyone about the lady," she said. "It was really on account of her that we forgot to watch the sheep."

"People wouldn't believe us if we did tell them," put in Francisco. "They'd say no lady ever stood on that little tree over there, all shining in white and gold."

"My mother would say I was lying," sighed Jacinta, "and then I'd get an awful scolding."

So it was decided to keep everything a secret—as had been done concerning the Angel of Peace, and that night, when Lucia left her cousins to go to her own home, she was almost walking on air. How fine to know that the beautiful lady would come again! And again and again!

"Five more times," she thought happily, "on the thirteenth day of June, July, August, September and October. Oh, how wonderful!"

Alas for the cherished secret! That night little Jacinta was too excited to sleep. She kept turning nervously in her bed, mumbling to herself in a strange fashion. Her eyes seemed unusually bright, and finally her mother grew fearful. Perhaps the child was coming down with a fever. And Francisco, too. He was not as restless as his sister, but there was something peculiar about his actions. He seemed to be in a kind of day-dream.

"Something's happened to you two!" said the mother sharply. "Tell me what it is!"

Confused and weary from the day's long strain, and upset by her mother's impatience, Jacinta finally broke down and sobbed out the whole story.

"We didn't do anything wrong, Mother. Only when the beautiful lady came . . ."

"What beautiful lady?"

"The lady in white and gold. She stood on top of a little tree in the Cova da Iria . . ."

"Yes," put in Francisco, "and she was very kind. But she said that I must offer many Rosaries before I can go to heaven . . ."

15

"We must all say the Rosary, very devoutly, every day. And we must suffer, too. Then sinners will be converted and the war will come to an end."

The mother's amazement knew no bounds. What nonsense was this? If Francisco and Jacinta had made up a weird tale just to attract attention to themselves...

"No, no!" cried the children, terrified of being punished. "Ask Lucia, Mother! She was with us! She can tell you everything is true!"

Chapter 3 The Lady Comes Again

HE NEXT morning the children's mother set out for Lucia's house, a little worried in spite of herself. Ever since breakfast Francisco and Jacinta had talked of nothing but the visit of the beautiful lady. More than that. They insisted that she was coming to see them again on the thirteenth day of June, the feast of Saint Anthony.

"How ridiculous!" thought the good woman. "When my sister-in-law hears of this foolishness, she'll be really angry."

Lucia's mother was angry when she learned of the apparition and lost no time in punishing her daughter for what she considered to be a willful falsehood.

"Don't ever lie to me again!" she cried angrily. "That's one fault my children have never had!"

In vain Lucia sobbed out that she was innocent. She hadn't told any lie. She and her cousins really had seen the lady.

"Then what's her name? And if she's so beautiful, why does she waste her time in a poor sheep pasture?"

The child wiped her tearful eyes. "The lady didn't tell us her name ... she's going to do that in October ... and I don't know why she came to the Cova da Iria. She ... she just *came!*"

Suddenly Lucia's mother reached a grim decision: this ten-year-old daughter was more stubborn than she had thought. The only thing to do was to take her to the parish priest, Father Marques Ferreira. Perhaps, after a good talking-to in Confession ...

"Yes," put in her sister-in-law, "and don't forget Francisco and Jacinta. They're too young to go to Confession, but I'll take them to the priest, too. I'll see that they tell him how bad they've been!"

So presently Lucia was brought before the parish priest, alone at first, then with Francisco and Jacinta. All three were very much afraid, but even so their story remained the same. Not even when their families threatened them with fresh punishments would they change a word.

"Dear God! What's going to become of us?" cried Lucia's mother frantically. "What will people say when they hear you talking like this?"

Father Ferreira smiled. He knew the three children very well. While he could not bring himself to believe everything they had told him concerning the beautiful lady, he did not think they were intentionally lying. Indeed, he explained the whole matter in a very simple way. The little ones were shepherds, weren't they? They spent long hours

THEIR STORY REMAINED THE SAME.

19

in the hills with their flocks? Well, what was more natural than that sometimes they should grow lonely, that they should wish for new friends, for exciting adventures? Not realizing what they had done, they had imagined a most wonderful and comforting friend: a beautiful lady in white and gold, who spoke to them about heaven, about saying the Rosary, about saving souls.

"Now the children have convinced themselves that their lady is real," he said kindly. "But they intend no lie. And of course they shouldn't be punished any more."

The two women were much relieved at the priest's words and returned home in a happier frame of mind.

"Father Ferreira's a wise man," said Lucia's mother. "I guess we should be guided by what he says."

"Yes, indeed," put in her sister-in-law comfortingly. "And it's not as though the children had lied to us. They didn't, you know. They only imagined the whole thing."

"Yes. But what do we do now?"

"Nothing, of course."

"*Nothing?* You mean that we should let them go to the Cova next month—on the thirteenth?"

"That's right. When they find that we pay no attention to their little game, they'll lose interest, too. Wait and see if I'm not right."

But Jacinta's mother was not right. As the days passed, the children became more interested than ever in the beautiful lady. They said the Rosary, and properly. There was no more skimming through the decades with only the first two words of the *Our Father* and the *Hail Mary*. They now understood that sinners would be saved and the terrible World War brought to a speedy end only through real prayer and sacrifice.

Suddenly, on the twelfth day of June, Lucia startled the other two children by announcing that she would not be going to the Cova for the lady's second visit. Instead, she would accompany her mother to the fair being held in honor of Saint Anthony at the neighboring village of Porto-de-Mos.

"I think we ought to celebrate Saint Anthony's feast as we've always done," she explained. "Why don't you come, too?"

The suggestion horrified Francisco and Jacinta. "How can you say such things?" they cried. "You know the lady told us to be at the Cova tomorrow."

"*The lady!* Do you know what I think?"

"What?"

"I think maybe the lady comes from hell."

"*Lucia!*"

"Yes. Maybe she's really the Devil, and we ought to leave her alone."

This was too much for seven-year-old Jacinta, and she began to cry as though her heart would break. How could such a beautiful lady be the Devil? It was a terrible thing to say!

Lucia put an arm about her little cousin. "Jacinta, please don't cry. I only said the lady *may* be the Devil. I didn't say she *is*. And if she asks for me tomorrow, tell her that I didn't come because I was afraid."

But Jacinta refused to be comforted, and finally Francisco spoke up. "You know we can't go without you, Lucia."

"Why not?"

"Because the lady doesn't speak to us. She speaks to you. Oh, we just couldn't go alone!"

Neither Jacinta's tears nor Francisco's arguments could change Lucia's mind, however, for she had not forgotten her mother's anger after the lady's first visit. "I don't want another beating," she declared firmly. "If you two want to go to the Cova tomorrow, you'll have to go alone."

Early the next morning the road leading from Fatima to Porto-de-Mos was dotted with lumbering farm wagons. These were piled high with fruit and vegetables, and gaily-dressed peasants walked beside them, laughing and singing. Yes, the whole countryside was in a festive mood, for this bright and sunny day was a national holiday, the feast of the great Saint Anthony, who had died in Padua in 1231 but who still belonged to Portugal, having been born in Lisbon in 1195.

Although she really had planned to go to the fair with the others, to take part in the games and dancing, Lucia suddenly changed her mind. Slowly and almost fearfully she set out for her cousins' house, for now she knew that she was going to the Cova after all. Indeed, something told her that it would be wrong to stay away, and soon this news was being imparted to Francisco and Jacinta.

The two children, whose family had left them for the gay events at Porto-de-Mos, were overjoyed when they saw their cousin. They had been almost sick with anxiety—afraid to go to the Cova without Lucia, afraid, too, to disobey the lady and remain at home.

"Well, now the three of us will go together," said Lucia comfortingly. "And we won't worry that others are going to the Cova, too."

"Others?" cried Francisco. "But I thought everyone in the village had gone to the fair!"

Lucia shook her head. "You know how people have talked about us," she said. "Now a good many have stayed away from the fair just to see if there really is a lady in the Cova."

Yes, about seventy people were grouped about the sheep pasture when the children arrived, including Lucia's father. For the most part they were talking and laughing, but they soon became silent as the youngsters approached a large tree, knelt down in its shade and began to recite the Rosary. Some even joined the children in prayer, but there were also those who remained apart and who winked slyly at one another.

"We'll soon see the end of this nonsense!" they seemed to say.

The little shepherds paid scant attention to the grown-ups who had come to watch them. Quietly and devoutly they offered their Rosary to the Queen of Heaven. Then, the prayer finished, Jacinta suggested that there might be time to offer another five mysteries. But Lucia shook her head, scrambled to her feet, and began to tidy her clothes.

"The lady is already here," she said. "Didn't you see the flash of light a little while ago?"

Amazed, Jacinta and Francisco turned to where their cousin pointed. Why, it was true! The lady had come to them again, just as she had promised! Right now she was standing atop the little holm-oak, dressed in shining white and gold, as spotless and as beautiful as on her visit of a month ago!

Eagerly the three ran toward her, unafraid this time, their hearts filled with a wonderful happiness. Lucia in particular could not control her joy.

"What do you want me to do?" she cried.

The lady's smile was gracious as she looked upon her little friend. "Continue to say the Rosary every day," she said gently, "and after the *Gloria* of each mystery, add these words: '*O Jesus, forgive us our sins! Save us from the fires of hell. Bring all souls to heaven, especially those who have most need of Your mercy!*'"

The lady's voice was like the most beautiful music, and Lucia and Jacinta thrilled at the sound. As for Francisco, he did not complain because he could not hear the words of the heavenly stranger. Somehow he believed that his former laziness at prayer, the many times he had neglected to say the Rosary, were alone responsible. Now he was more than grateful that at least the lady allowed herself to be visible to him, that she had shown him the importance of the Rosary, that at long last he was beginning to understand something of its wonderful power to bring souls to God.

The minutes passed, and the lady continued to speak to Lucia. She informed her that she must learn to read, also that she and her little cousins must remember to pray for sinners.

"Many souls go to hell because there is no one to pray and make sacrifices for them," she said gravely.

Hell! Suddenly there was real terror in Lucia's heart, and she cried out that she was afrail of this terrible place, that she wished the lady to take her to heaven—and at once! Surely this was possible, since the beautiful one had already said that she lived there.

"And take Jacinta and Francisco, too!" she begged. *"Please!"*

The vision nodded. "I will take them soon, but you must remain here for some time yet."

Poor Lucia! These words filled her with sadness, and she could have shed bitter tears. Yet somehow there were no tears, for the lady's loving gaze held her as she began to speak again, and of something both strange and wonderful.

"My Son has work for you to do," she said. "He wants to make use of you to establish devotion to my Immaculate Heart."

Puzzled, the ten-year-old girl stared up into the face of the apparition. Surely there must be some mistake! How could the lady expect her to do any work, once Francisco and Jacinta had been taken to heaven? As for the Immaculate Heart— *what was that?*

24

Chapter 4 — The Message

THE LADY sensed Lucia's bewilderment. Indeed, when the little girl complained at having to stay in the world without her beloved cousins, she hastened to comfort her in a kind and motherly way.

"No, no, my child. You will not be alone. I will never abandon you. My Immaculate Heart will be your refuge and the way that will lead you to Jesus."

As she spoke, the lady stretched out her hands, and suddenly all three children experienced a thrill of pure joy. It seemed as though bright rays of light extended from the lady's hands to their own hearts, rays which brought with them a love and warmth they had never felt before. Now, how easy to know and love the Immaculate Heart. Why, it was the Heart of the Blessed Virgin, and God wished them to make this Most Pure Heart known and loved by others!

As though to confirm this the lady suddenly pointed to herself, whereupon all three children saw her heart, surrounded by great thorns that wounded it from every side. Then, her eyes upon Lucia, the beautiful one began to speak:

"My child, behold my heart surrounded with the thorns which ungrateful men place therein at every moment by their blasphemies and ingratitude. You, at least, try to console me."

The little girl clasped her hands. How cruelly the thorns pressed into the lady's heart! No wonder there was such pain in her eyes, in her voice! Oh, if only there was something she and her cousins could do to relieve her suffering! But suddenly the lady was speaking again, in slow and solemn tones:

"Make known to men that I promise to assist at the hour of death, with the graces necessary for salvation, all those who, on the first Saturday of five consecutive months, go to Confession, receive Holy Communion, say the Rosary, and spend a quarter of an hour with me in meditating on the fifteen mysteries of the Rosary, with the object of making reparation to me."

It was a strange and wonderful message, and Lucia's eyes shone with joy as its full meaning dawned upon her. Yet there was regret in her heart, too, for well she knew that Francisco and Jacinta could not share fully in this new work. They had not made their First Communion in the parish church, and so of course they would not be allowed to receive the Holy Eucharist on the first Saturday of each month. But even as Lucia was considering this problem, the beautiful lady suddenly turned toward the east, glided swiftly from the branches of the little holm-oak and disappeared into thin air.

For a long moment the three children stared forlornly after her. Then, understanding that their heavenly friend

"YOU, AT LEAST, TRY TO CONSOLE ME."

had really left them for another month, that now it was time to offer new prayers and sacrifices for sinners, they arose from their knees.

"That lady is so beautiful!" sighed Jacinta, gazing wistfully across the sheep pasture. "But the dreadful thorns in her heart! Why are they there, Lucia? Why does she have to suffer so much?"

The child hesitated. "Don't you remember? She said that sinners put the thorns there. Oh, Jacinta, we must do everything we can to comfort her! We must say the Rosary as perfectly as possible."

"Yes, of course. But I don't understand how anyone could bear to hurt such a beautiful lady."

"I don't, either. Yet you heard what she said—and you saw the thorns. Surely if we try very hard to be good, at least we can help to make up for what *one* sinner is doing to the lady."

Suddenly nine-year-old Francisco grew restless. Weren't the two girls going to tell him what had taken place during the lady's visit? Surely they hadn't forgotten that he could not hear one word of the heavenly visitor's conversation!

"Tell me everything!" he begged. "Please!"

A wave of compassion swept through Lucia's heart. Poor Francisco! What a pity that he could not hear the lady's beautiful voice!

"The most important thing today was the part about the Five First Saturdays," she hastened to explain. "The lady wants people to go to Confession and Communion on these days, Francisco."

"The lady did say just that," interrupted Jacinta, her eyes very wide and serious. "And she also said that if people do this five times in a row, and say the Rosary, and spend fifteen minutes thinking about the different mysteries, the

Blessed Virgin will come to them when they are dying and help them go to heaven."

"But they must do these things to console her Immaculate Heart," added Lucia, "in reparation for sinners. Do you know what reparation means, Francisco?"

The boy nodded. "Reparation" was a long word, but the lady used it a great deal in her talks with Lucia. It meant making up for other people's sins by extra and more fervent prayer—also by suffering. And it was not just something expected of older people. Children, even very little children, could make reparation. Every day in the week they could help to make up for the sins of others by being cheerful, obedient, willing.

"Yes, I understand about reparation," said Francisco. "For me, it's come to mean saying the Rosary properly. But once I've made my First Communion, I'll go to Confession and Communion on the first Saturday of every month, too."

"So will I," chimed in Jacinta. "Oh, how sad I feel when I think of the lazy way I used to say Our Lady's prayer! Maybe many poor sinners went to hell because I didn't try hard enough to help them!"

"The lady also told us that we must love the Immaculate Heart of the Blessed Virgin very, very much," said Lucia. "When she saw that we didn't have this love, she stretched out her hands towards us, and bright rays of light came out from them and warmed our hearts. Don't you remember them, Francisco? And don't you love the Blessed Virgin very much now?"

The boy nodded. Of course he remembered the rays. And of course he now loved the Blessed Virgin—in a new and wonderful way.

The children were so lost in their discussion of reparation that at first they did not notice the many curious onlookers drifting toward them from the outskirts of the pasture. But suddenly the air was filled with the sound of babbling tongues. Had the lady come as she had promised? If so, why hadn't seventy pairs of good Christian eyes been able to see her?

Suddenly the old fear was upon Lucia. She knew that her father was present somewhere in the crowd, also a few of her mother's friends. If she was not careful, there might be much foolish gossip later on about the morning's happenings. People would misunderstand. Back in Fatima there would be talk of lies, of deceit, of a ten-year-old girl who was setting herself up as an important person by claiming to see visions. Then, even though it was Saint Anthony's feast day, this same ten-year-old girl knew that she could expect to be severely punished when her mother arrived home from the fair at Porto-de-Mos.

Suddenly determined to say as little as possible, and not a word about the Immaculate Heart, (since the lady had warned they must keep this part of her conversation a secret for the time being), Lucia pointed resolutely to the small holm-oak.

"The lady came a little while ago. She stood over there."

"On top of that poor little tree?"

"Yes. Just like the last time."

"And what did she have to say?"

"She taught us a prayer to be said after the *Gloria* of each mystery of the Rosary."

"Do you remember the prayer?"

"*O Jesus, forgive us our sins! Save us from the fires of hell. Bring all souls to heaven, especially those who have most need of Your mercy!*"

For a moment there was silence as the crowd pondered the touching words of the prayer.

"Didn't the lady say anything else?" someone asked curiously.

"Yes, she gave me a message. But it's a secret, and we're not to tell anyone without her permission."

Suddenly a hard-headed farmer from nearby Aljustrel broke into a hearty laugh. "You're quite an actress, Lucia! For a while you really had me fooled!"

"Yes, all three play their parts well," scoffed another. "Who taught you how to act like this, children?"

The little shepherds looked about in amazement and pain. Oh, no! Surely these friends and neighbors didn't think they were deceiving them! Surely they weren't going to make fun of the visits of a lady from heaven!

"Let's go now," whispered Jacinta, "and quickly, before anyone tries to stop us."

So the three joined hands and started to run across the pasture to the highway. But they had gone only a short distance when an elderly peasant woman appeared from behind a clump of bushes and stood directly in their path. Clearly she had guessed the children's plans to return home by this route and had been waiting for them.

"Don't be frightened," she said kindly. "I'm not like the others. I really believe in your lady. Won't you tell me what else she said to you this morning?"

The children stopped. Could it be that here was someone who would not make fun of them, who perhaps would be willing to pray and make sacrifices for sinners?

"The lady gave us a secret message which we are not to breathe to a soul—that is, until she says we may," said Lucia cautiously.

"Yes, child. I heard you saying this before. But didn't she tell you anything else?"

"She told us to say the Rosary often and to add the special prayer after the *Gloria* of each mystery."

"And then?"

"She said to pray, to pray much and make sacrifices for sinners, that many souls are going to hell because there are none to make sacrifices and to pray for them."

The woman listened to the words of the heavenly visitor with tears in her eyes. Then she looked lovingly at the children. Now she would explain why she so firmly believed that their lady had stood atop the little holm-oak that morning. After all, it was the real reason that she had slipped away from the crowd and waited for them here.

"I came to the pasture early today with some friends," she began. "We had heard the story about the lady who spoke to you last month and how she was supposed to come again today, and so we made sure that we were at the Cova in plenty of time."

"The lady is coming next month, too," put in Jacinta eagerly, "on the thirteenth of July."

"Yes, I know. But listen, child. While we were waiting for the three of you to arrive, my friends and I walked all about the little holm-oak. We examined it very carefully, and we noticed that the top was covered with folded buds. These were very firm, and they were pointing directly to the sky. But after you had prayed and talked to your lady, what do you think happened?"

A soft glow came into Lucia's eyes. "What?" she whispered.

Slowly the peasant woman made the Sign of the Cross. "All the buds were bent to one side! Yes, to the east, as though the lady's long mantle had trailed over them when she went away! Oh, my children, how can anyone fail to believe in the lady now? Surely even a fool must know that she *is*, and that the message she brings to us comes from heaven!"

Chapter 5 — A New Life

¶N ONE sense the peasant woman was right. After the second of the lady's apparitions, many in Fatima began to believe in her. Indeed, the story of what had taken place in the Cova da Iria spread like wildfire, and on the thirteenth day of July, the date set by the lady for her third appearance, more than five thousand people were on hand at the sheep pasture.

Once again the children knelt and recited the five mysteries of the Rosary, inserting at the end of each decade the prayer previously taught them by the lady. Then came the blinding flash of light, and the three turned joyfully toward the small holm-oak. Yes—their heavenly friend had come again! She was standing atop the little tree, and she was as bright and beautiful as the noon-day sun!

"What do you want of us?" cried Lucia eagerly, heedless of the fact that this time five thousand people were watching her every movement, listening to her every word.

The lady smiled. "I want you to continue saying the Rosary every day in honor of the Blessed Virgin," she said gently. "Only she can bring an end to this terrible war."

"But who are *you*, please? So many people want to know!"

The lady's eyes were kind. "In October I will tell you who I am. Continue coming here on the thirteenth day of each month until then. And tell those who do not believe that in October I will work a great miracle that will convince them I am real."

After they had recited the Rosary, the lady stretched out her hands as she had done during the second apparition, and once again the children saw that bright rays came forth from the fingertips. But almost immediately their eyes filled with horror, for this time the heavenly light was not directed toward them but toward the ground, and of a sudden the earth seemed to vanish, and they found themselves standing at the edge of a vast and fiery ocean.

As they peered down into this dreadful place, the terrified children saw huge numbers of devils and damned souls. The devils resembled hideous black animals, each filling the air with despairing shrieks. The damned souls were in their human bodies and seemed to be brown in color, tumbling constantly about in the flames and screaming with terror. All were on fire, within and without their bodies, and neither devils nor damned souls seemed able to control their movements. They were tossing about in the flame like fiery coals in a furnace. There was never an instant's peace or freedom from pain.

FIVE THOUSAND PEOPLE WERE ON HAND.

35

Just as quickly as it had come, the terrifying vision suddenly melted away and the children found themselves in the world once more—in the reassuring and familiar surroundings of the sheep pasture. As the lady looked at the three little shepherds, her eyes were dark with grief.

"You have just seen hell, where the souls of sinners will suffer forever," she said. "To save other souls from going there, God wants to establish in the world the devotion to my Immaculate Heart. If people will do what I tell you, many souls will be saved, and there will be peace."

How reverently the children listened to the sweet and sorrowful voice—and how gratefully—for it was certain that they could not have looked longer at the dreadful vision of hell without dying of terror.

"The war[1] will end," continued the lady. "But if people do not cease to offend God, a worse one will break out in the reign of the next Pope.[2] When you see a night illuminated by an unknown light[3], know that this is the great sign given you by God that He is about to punish the world for its crimes by means of war, famine, and persecutions of the Church and of the Holy Father.

"To avoid such a calamity, I come to ask the consecration of the world to my Immaculate Heart and also the Communion in reparation on the first Saturday of each month. If the world heeds my requests, Russia will be converted and there will be peace. If the world does not heed my requests, this country will spread its errors throughout the

---

[1] The First World War, 1914-1918.
[2] Pius the Eleventh, 1922-39.
[3] This is believed to have taken place on the night of January 24-25, 1938, when a very unusual Aurora Borealis was seen in all Europe and North America.

world, promoting wars and persecutions of the Church. Then the faithful will become martyrs; the Holy Father will have much to suffer; various nations will be destroyed. But in the end my Immaculate Heart will triumph. The Holy Father will consecrate Russia to me; it will be converted, and some time of peace will be conceded to the world."

It was the longest speech the lady had ever made, and when she had disappeared as usual, the children were trembling with fear. How terrible had been the vision of hell! Oh, surely nothing worse could befall a person than that God's Justice should condemn him to this horrible place forever!

Suddenly a man's mocking voice rang through the Cova. "Well, what happened this time? Did your wonderful lady come and talk to you?"

There was a gasp of indignation from his wife. "Of course she came! Didn't you see how the little holm-oak was surrounded with a strange light?"

"It was like shining dust! The tree and the children were surrounded with shining dust!" cried an old woman. "I saw it! And I could hear Lucia speaking to somebody, too! Oh, this *is* a holy place!"

"Nonsense! The priest is paying these children to make fools of us!"

"Watch your tongue! The priest isn't even here today."

"And why not? So that no one will suspect him of anything. Oh, he's a clever one, that priest of Fatima . . . "

So the tongues wagged, and soon five thousand people, including the children's families, were milling about the pasture in a state of high excitement. The parents of Jacinta and Francisco were less upset than might have been expected, but it was a different story with Lucia's mother.

"Look!" she cried, pointing toward the little holm-oak. "People are kneeling in that place as though it was a holy shrine! Oh, just wait until I get my hands on Lucia! Why, the Devil himself must be in her, to make her act as though she was good enough to see visions!"

"But Father Ferreira said the children weren't to be punished," warned her sister-in-law. "Don't you remember? He said they were only imagining things."

"Imagining! Lucia won't be imagining things tonight. Wait and see!"

It was true. Before very long Lucia's mother had given her another beating. More than that. The child's four sisters and brother, far from sympathizing with her, had made her understand that she was bringing disgrace upon the family by her actions. For instance, if there really was a lady in the Cova, why couldn't everyone see her—not just three silly children who didn't even know how to read and write?

"Confess that it's all a lie," urged one of the girls. "Then there'll be no more trouble for you."

"Yes, and I can have some peace," grumbled the brother. "Why, now I can't even stir out of the house without someone pointing at me and whispering."

Poor Lucia! She loved her family very much and would have gone through many hardships to make them happy. But deny the lady's visits, the conversations with her, the message that people must change their lives, say the Rosary every day and cultivate a deep devotion to the Immaculate Heart of the Blessed Virgin? Oh, no! This was quite impossible. It meant telling a lie. And Lucia knew that to tell a lie is one of the ugliest sins a child can commit. No good can ever come from it.

"But I still wish Mother would understand!" she thought tearfully. "It's so hard to know that I'm making her unhappy and that she doesn't trust me any more. And how I dread the beatings and scoldings!"

In the days that followed, Francisco and Jacinta did their best to comfort Lucia, for they realized how she was suffering. Indeed, they also were in difficulties because of the lady, since now many pilgrims were coming long distances to pray at the Cova, to leave offerings of money before the little holm-oak. Without fail, all of these people wanted to see and speak with the three young shepherds before returning home—a practice that caused as much annoyance to Francisco's mother as it did to her sister-in-law.

"But we ought to be glad in one way," said seven-year-old Jacinta. "And you ought to be glad, too, Lucia, that your mother beats and scolds you. Oh, how I wish my parents would do that to me!"

Lucia's eyes widened. "Jacinta! How can you say such a thing?"

"Because then I would have many new sacrifices to offer to Our Lord. Oh, Lucia! Surely you haven't forgotten that terrible vision of hell?"

The child shuddered. "Of course not! It was too awful to forget."

"Then don't forget what the lady said, either: about how many people have gone there because there was no one to pray and to make sacrifices in reparation for their sins."

"I know. I think about sinners every day."

"Then offer up the beatings and scoldings to God. Maybe they'll be enough to keep one person out of hell."

"Yes, and *we* can do things, too," put in Francisco eagerly. "We can make many little sacrifices that no one will notice."

So presently the three children were entering upon a new life, a life of prayer and suffering for others. Jacinta was the leader in this venture, and Lucia and Francisco marveled at the many ways she discovered for them to do penance for sinners. One day they were to go without a drink of cold water when thirsty. On another, they were to give away their lunches to some poor children and content themselves with eating the bitter acorns to be found in the pasture. Most important of all: they were to be cheerful and obedient at home, for God expected this of them before any other service.

One day the three were discussing the message which the lady had brought them on her third and most recent visit—the message that was to be kept a secret until she herself gave the word to pass it on to others.

"How awful to know that unless people change their lives there'll be another war!" said Jacinta sadly. "Oh, Lucia! I think about this so much!"

"So do I," put in Francisco. "And about Russia, too. Lucia, the lady said she wants this country consecrated to her Immaculate Heart so that it can be converted. Does that mean it's a wicked country now?"

The child shook her head. "I don't know. But I remember what the lady said: 'If the world does not heed my requests, this country will spread its errors throughout the world, promoting wars and persecutions of the Church. Then the faithful will become martyrs; the Holy Father will have much to suffer; various nations will be destroyed.' "

"It doesn't sound as though it was a very good place," muttered Jacinta. "Probably only a few people there ever say the Rosary properly."

"But why?" cried Francisco. "Don't they know how much happier they'd be if they'd love Our Lady?"

These words made Lucia start. What a change had come over Francisco—and over Jacinta and herself as well! Only a few short months ago they had prayed chiefly from a sense of duty. There had been but a small amount of love in their prayers, or joy. Now, what a difference! Because the lady had stretched out her hands to them and warmed them with the wonderful rays, they longed to pray as much as possible and to suffer for sinners. And it was impossible to think that they could ever again let a day go by without saying the Rosary!

"Maybe other people could have this grace, too, if only they would ask the lady for it," thought the little girl. "Even the people in Russia. Oh, how wonderful that would be!"

LUCIA'S thoughts were wiser than she knew. In July, 1917, there was a really great need that the Russian people should recite the Rosary devoutly, for within three months Communism was to sweep over the land and cause untold misery to millions. In a lesser degree this was true of other European countries—including Portugal, where since 1910 atheists had been in firm control of the government.

Atheists! One of these was the mayor of Ourem (the nearest town of any size to Fatima), and when word was brought to him of the miraculous happenings in the Cova, he was beside himself with rage.

"You mean that three little peasants are setting themselves up as *prophets?*" he roared. "What nonsense! Don't waste my time or yours with such fairy tales!"

Respectfully the mayor's assistants informed him that events at Fatima could not be ignored. Some five thousand people had gone to the Cova da Iria for the lady's appearance in July. Possibly three times this number, or even more, would be on hand in August, for the apparitions had been given wide publicity in the newspapers. Everyone was interested.

"Well, I'm not interested," said the mayor bluntly. "You know I don't believe in God. Then why should I believe in silly visions that tell me to say the Rosary?"

"Perhaps you should be interested," suggested an assistant slyly. "After all, Fatima is in territory under your control. If there's any disturbance there next month ..."

"Yes, fifteen thousand people could make trouble if they became excited," put in a deputy. "It wouldn't look well, sir, if the government in Lisbon found out that you hadn't taken precautions."

The mayor snorted. "Well, what do you want me to do?"

The deputy and the assistants swiftly agreed on one point: the mayor must order the three children of Fatima and their fathers to appear before him at Ourem. Being of peasant stock, these simple folk would be much afraid of any officer of the law. With a little coaxing they could be made to confess that the whole affair was a fraud, that the parish priest had ordered them to begin a shrine that would rival the famous grotto at Lourdes and thus bring both pilgrims and prominence to Fatima.

"You see, sir, there's nothing more to it than this," explained the assistant. "These peasants wanted to make some extra money. So, when the priest promised them a share in what the future pilgrims would leave ..."

"Exactly!" broke in the deputy. "I've always felt that religion is a cleverly organized business. Now I know it. The sooner we can close every church in Portugal, as we have done with the convents and seminaries, the sooner we

43

can have an extra source of income and less taxes for ourselves. That's the way it is in a really up-to-date country." The mayor's crafty eyes lit up. "I do believe you're right," he said. "If we can do something up here in the hills to kill religion ... "

"And we can, sir. Every little bit helps."

"Of course. Go, order these stupid children and their fathers to come to Ourem at once. Let them see that we understand their little game."

So a message was despatched to Fatima, announcing that Antonio dos Santos, father of Lucia, and Manuel Marto, father of Francisco and Jacinta, must appear before the mayor of Ourem. And they were to bring the children with them.

Surprisingly enough, Manuel Marto was far from fearful over the unexpected summons. Calmly he declared that he would go to Ourem and answer whatever questions the mayor cared to ask. But he would not bring Francisco and Jacinta. They were too young to make such a tiring trip.

"Leave Lucia at home, too," he advised his brother-in-law. "After all, what harm has the child done?"

But Lucia's mother would not hear of this. "The girl goes with you," she informed her husband. "Didn't she start this whole affair in the first place?"

Lucia was most unhappy that she had to go to Ourem without her cousins. Yet when the time came for her to tell her story to the mayor, she spoke up bravely. Yes—there was a heavenly lady in the Cova. She would make herself seen for the fourth time on the thirteenth day of August. So far her message had been that people must change their lives, say the Rosary and make sacrifices for sinners.

"And when the lady came last month she taught us a new prayer," the child concluded. "Every time we make a sacrifice for sinners we are to say it."

LUCIA WAS MOST UNHAPPY WITHOUT HER COUSINS.

The mayor's face grew hard. "Yes? And what's this prayer?"

" 'Oh, my Jesus, I offer this for the love of Thee, for the conversion of sinners, and in reparation for all the wrongs done to the Immaculate Heart of Mary.' "

These holy words were too much for the mayor, whose heart had long been set against God and religion. "Silly little girl!" he cried. "If you want to be punished, just keep on with such stupid lies as these!"

"But they're not lies, sir. We really saw the beautiful lady. And she really said everything I've told you."

"Nonsense! There is no lady. And you must give me your solemn promise not to go to the Cova on the thirteenth of August. Come, now—hurry up!"

Lucia looked imploringly at her father, at her uncle, knowing only too well that they could do little for her. Then, folding her hands, she spoke in a firm but respectful voice:

"I can't promise not to go to the Cova on the thirteenth."

"Why not?"

"Because the lady said we were to be there that day, and we have to obey her. After all, she comes from heaven."

In vain the mayor threatened, coaxed, threatened again. He could not obtain the promise he desired so much. Nor could he force from Lucia the smallest part of the secret message she and her cousins had been given in July.

"Well, why don't *you* do something?" he cried finally, turning to the father and uncle who had been standing by, silent witnesses of his futile efforts. "After all, this stubborn child is yours—not mine!"

Antonio dos Santos and Manuel Marto shrugged their shoulders. What could they do? Lucia had her faults, but telling lies was not one of them—or breaking promises, either. Besides, weeks ago others had tried to make the girl change her story. There had been scoldings, beatings, even several interviews with the parish priest. All to no avail.

Abruptly, the mayor gave in and ordered the three peasants to leave his office. But even as they made their way back to Fatima, an evil scheme was brewing in his mind.

"That stubborn little girl wouldn't give me her promise not to go to the Cova," he thought. "That means she and the others will be there on the thirteenth of August. They'll pretend the heavenly lady came and talked to them once more, and thousands of stupid pilgrims will go into hysterics. But," and there was a cruel gleam in the mayor's eyes, "it *could* be a different story—*if the children were kept away from the Cova by force!*"

The more he thought, the more the mayor was convinced that he had hit upon the perfect plan to put an end to the unusual happenings at Fatima. It would be so easy to kidnap the children! On the thirteenth day of August, just as they were setting out for the Cova, he would drive up to their house in his shiny black automobile. He would be very kind and gracious. He would even apologize for his previous harsh words. Then he would beg the parents' permission to drive the three children to the sheep pasture. He would assure them that he believed in the heavenly lady and that he wished to be on hand at the Cova as a pilgrim. Surely they couldn't refuse him permission to escort the children in his car, especially since he was doing it in a spirit of reparation?

A little before eleven o'clock on the thirteenth day of August, the mayor put the first part of his unholy plan into action. With a grand flourish he drove up to the Marto house, where the children and their families were assembled, and asked permission to take Lucia, Francisco and Jacinta to the Cova. It was a hot day, he said, and more than a mile to the sheep pasture. Surely the children would be very tired if they had to walk the entire distance, and on a road crowded with pilgrims?

The Marto and dos Santos families were surprised—and not a little pleased—that the mayor of Ourem should come to their door and ask a favor. After a short conference, the two fathers gave the desired permission. Then as they stood there, somewhat fascinated at the sight of the shiny black automobile, the mayor settled the children inside the machine and gave orders to be off.

The three little shepherds would have much preferred walking to the Cova, but they dared not question their parents' wishes. However, it was not long before Lucia was looking up anxiously at the mayor.

"Please, sir, we're going the wrong way. The Cova is back of us, not in front."

The latter chuckled. "I know. But I thought we'd make a quick trip to Ourem. I want the three of you to meet the parish priest there."

Francisco's eyes were wide with alarm. "*Ourem?* But we haven't time, sir! The lady always comes about noon. Please turn back!"

"Oh, yes!" cried Jacinta. "It would be just terrible if we were late!"

Once again the mayor smiled his crafty smile. "Don't you know anything about automobiles, children? Why, we can go to Ourem and still be at the Cova in plenty of time for your lady."

For several minutes all was silence as the car sped along the highway. Then the outline of Ourem came into view, and Lucia's eyes brightened as they noted a nearby steeple glistening in the sun. The church! Why, this trip hadn't taken so long after all! Probably the parish priest lived

48

only a few steps away, and they could see him at once. Then, what joy! They could be on their way back to Fatima. Once more the lady would stand atop the holm-oak. She would smile, would encourage her little friends to pray and make sacrifices for sinners. Perhaps there might even be a new message ...

Suddenly Lucia's blood ran cold. The car had shot past the church, past the priest's house, and now was slowing up before an imposing and familiar building. As the child turned to the mayor, her eyes were dark with suspicion.

"This isn't the priest's house!"

"No? What is it then?"

"It's where *you* live ... "

The man laughed harshly. "So you remember it from your first visit, do you? Well, remember this, too, my girl. It's also the jail, and full of thieves and murderers. Come, now—out with the three of you!"

The jail! Francisco and Jacinta cringed as the mayor jerked them from the car. Oh, what was going to happen? What was this terrible man going to do?

SOON the little shepherds' worst fears were realized. Since they would not deny that they had seen a heavenly lady, they were to be put in prison. Later, if they still insisted on being stubborn, there would be other punishments.

"That's the only way to treat such wicked children!" snapped the mayor. "Come along! Into this cell with you!"

The three stared at one another in dismay, for the cell before which the mayor had stopped was filled with prisoners—rough-looking men whose bearded faces bore the stamp of evil.

"Why, we've got company!" cried one suddenly, as the heavy barred door opened, then slammed behind the children. "And what company!"

"Yes!" jeered another. "Since when do they send us babies?"

"Oh, but these aren't babies! They're pickpockets—good ones. I remember the boy well."

"That's right. And I saw one of the girls at the fair in June. Come here, little ones. Tell us how they caught you."

"Yes. Speak up, children. You're among friends now."

Loud laughter greeted this remark, and for a moment the youngsters stood by the door in silent bewilderment. Then Lucia took courage. No, she and her cousins were not pickpockets—or any other kind of criminal. Instead, the three of them were from the country, and they had seen a heavenly lady. They had seen her three times, and she had promised to come again today. On each of her visits, she had asked the children to say the Rosary devoutly and to make many sacrifices for sinners. She had also told them a secret, but as yet they could not share this with anyone.

The prisoners stared in amazement. What nonsense was this? Then one man shook a warning finger at Lucia. "Don't make the mayor angry, little girl. He can cause you lots of trouble."

"Yes," put in another. "And don't talk to him about heavenly things. Bother him with some other kind of story."

Jacinta twisted her hands nervously. "But sir! We never make up *any* stories!"

"That's right," hastened Francisco. "And even if the mayor leaves us here forever, we can't say that we never saw the lady."

There was something touching in the children's honest speech and bearing, and in spite of themselves the prisoners were impressed. Suddenly they felt as though a clean breeze had swept through their dismal quarters, bringing with it a certain freshness and cheer. Later, when Jacinta took a medal from her neck and asked one of the men to hang it for her on a nail in the wall, he did so with a good grace.

"But why don't you want to keep on wearing the medal?" he asked curiously.

The child's eyes were solemn. "It must be noon now," she explained. "If we were at the Cova, the lady would be talking to us and asking us to say the Rosary. But perhaps she can hear us if we say it here in front of the medal, and be just as pleased."

As she spoke, the little girl knelt down—hands folded, eyes raised to the medal on the wall above her head. Her cousins and a few of the men did likewise, and soon the prison cell was echoing to an unusual sound: childish trebles telling the praises of the Blessed Virgin, accompanied by a faltering chorus of deep-pitched voices. Even those who took no part in the little service listened respectfully, for a certain spell had been cast upon the motley group by the young strangers from Fatima. There was no doubt about it, they told themselves. These were remarkable children. They really believed that a heavenly lady had told them to recite the Rosary daily, so that God's anger at a sinful world might be appeased!

Some time later, when the mayor returned to the cell, he was beside himself with disappointment. Far from denying the apparitions of the heavenly lady, the children were as strong as ever in their faith. More than that. They had now made friends with several of the prisoners, and for recreation Jacinta had even been dancing with one of them!

"We'll soon put a stop to this!" he fumed. "You won't be so sure of yourselves when you come to live with *me!*"

The mayor's living quarters were not far away, and presently the children found themselves locked in another large and dreary room.

THE PRISON ECHOED TO AN UNUSUAL SOUND.

"What's he going to do?" Francisco asked fearfully. Lucia shook her head. "I don't know. Maybe he'll beat us."

"If he does, we must remember the prayer," said Jacinta, "the one that the lady taught us to say whenever we make a sacrifice for sinners. Let's go over it now, shall we?"

So the three little ones knelt down and recited the familiar words: "Oh, my Jesus, I offer this for the love of Thee, for the conversion of sinners, and in reparation for all the wrongs done to the Immaculate Heart of Mary."

But although the children waited, their minds full of dreadful imaginings, the mayor did not return to beat them. His wife arrived instead—a good soul who was plainly distressed over her husband's cruelty. She brought food and drink to the three little prisoners and comforted them in a truly motherly fashion, but as twilight came on she was forced to admit that there was not much she could do that would be of real help.

"You mean, we have to stay here all night?" asked Jacinta, blinking back the tears.

"I'm afraid so, dear."

"And all day tomorrow?"

"Probably."

"And the next day, too?"

"I guess so."

This was discouraging news indeed. Two whole days away from home! Never had the children been absent so long from their families, and little Jacinta found it hard to keep from crying. How was she going to get along without her mother? But this first grief was destined to increase, for two days passed, then three days, four days, and still she and her cousins were kept prisoners in the mayor's house.

"Maybe we'll never go home!" she sobbed despairingly. "Oh, Lucia! What are we going to do? And why don't our parents come for us?"

Lucia was silent. Already the mayor had explained why no one had come for them. It was because they had disgraced their families by telling so many dreadful lies. Now, he assured them gloatingly, they did not have a single friend left in the whole village of Fatima.

"But maybe he was only trying to frighten us," she thought. "Maybe somebody will come tomorrow." Then aloud to Jacinta: "I don't know why nobody comes. But we can still offer this sacrifice for the conversion of sinners. You do want to, don't you?"

"Yes," urged Francisco. "Think of the glimpse we had of hell, Jacinta. And remember that the lady did say we would have much to suffer."

With a little sigh, Jacinta nodded and folded her hands. "With all my heart I want to offer this sacrifice," she murmured. "Oh, my Jesus, I offer this for the love of Thee, for the conversion of sinners, and in reparation for all the wrongs done to the Immaculate Heart of Mary!"

The next day—the fifth of the imprisonment—the mayor was forced to admit that the three little shepherds had overcome all his attempts to break down their story or to gain the least hint as to the nature of the secret which the lady had entrusted to them. Half beside himself with rage, he determined to make one last effort.

"Listen to me!" he roared, bursting into the room where the three were sitting listlessly by the window. "Either tell the truth about this lady, or each of you will be fried in oil!"

The man's face was twisted with fury, and the children drew back in alarm as he strode toward them. "But sir! We've already told you the truth!"

"The truth! Listen, you stubborn creatures! I've had enough nonsense. There's a big kettle of oil boiling on the stove this very minute, just right to cook the three of you to a crisp. Hurry up, Francisco. What's this secret you say the lady told you?"

The nine-year-old boy trembled with fear. "I can't tell you, sir."

"You can't? We'll see about that. Come on—out to the kitchen with you."

As the mayor seized her brother in an iron grip, Jacinta gasped with horror. Francisco was going to be fried in oil! "Oh, Lucia!" she cried, her face pale, her whole body tense with fright. "What are we going to do?"

The ten-year-old girl did not answer. By now the door had slammed shut and she was waiting to hear Francisco's screams as he was plunged into the boiling oil. But the minutes passed, and all was silence. Then suddenly the door opened, and the mayor strode into the room once more. His eyes were glittering.

"Well, that's one of you fried," he declared briskly, wiping his hands. "Now, my little Jacinta, it's your turn. Tell me your secret, or you go into the boiling oil, too."

By now great tears were running down the child's cheeks. "I can't tell the secret to anyone," she moaned. "I can't! I can't!"

The mayor did not bother to argue. With a harsh laugh he seized Jacinta by the arm and dragged her from the room. His face was livid with rage. Never before had stupid peasants dared to defy him.

Poor Lucia! When the door had slammed a second time and she found herself alone, her heart shrank with fear. To be fried in boiling oil! What a horrible death for Francisco, for little Jacinta! Quickly she fell upon her knees, filled with terror at the thought of the death that soon would be hers.

"Because I can't tell the secret either," she muttered. "No matter what the mayor does to me, I can't be untrue to the lady!"

Five minutes passed, ten minutes, and there was no sound from the kitchen. Suddenly Lucia could bear the strain no longer, and stretched forth her arms to heaven. She could not see the beautiful one whom she loved so much, but surely if she prayed to her ... if she asked for strength and courage ...

"Dear lady, please look after me!" she whispered. "Help me to die bravely ... like Francisco and Jacinta ... without a sound!"

Chapter 8 — The fourth Visit

VEN as Lucia offered this heartfelt prayer, the door opened and the mayor appeared.

"All right," he sneered cruelly. "Now it's your turn to die!"

The little girl was trembling like a leaf, but she did not cry out as the mayor dragged her toward the kitchen. Her mind could hold no other thoughts than these: her beloved cousins were dead. They had given their lives rather than be false to the lady. Now she must do the same.

The mayor flung open the kitchen door and Lucia gathered up all her courage to look upon the frightful scene. But even as she looked in she gasped, unable to believe her eyes. There, sitting in the kitchen with the mayor's wife were Francisco and Jacinta—white with fear but unharmed!

"Lucia, there isn't any boiling oil!" cried the little boy, rushing forward eagerly. "He was only trying to frighten us."

Jacinta was close behind her brother. "Yes. He thought we'd never really want to die for the lady. But we were ready to do it. You were, too, weren't you?"

As though in a dream, Lucia nodded. Then she burst into happy tears. "I was dreadfully afraid, but I'd rather have died a thousand times than disobey the lady!" she sobbed. "She's so kind and good."

The mayor was outraged at these words, but he knew that he was defeated. Soon he was hustling the three little shepherds into his automobile. "Stupid brats! You've wasted nearly a week of my time!" he roared. "Get back to your families and never bother me again with your silly stories!"

As the mayor's car speeded them along the highway from Ourem to Fatima, the children began to readjust themselves to the everyday world. It was now August 18, and they had been in prison for five days. The lady's visit (if she had come) was over and done with. But after the first stab of sorrow, they began to put the past behind them and to look forward to what awaited them in Fatima. How good to be going home at last! To be with their families and friends once again!

"I wonder if the lady came while we were away," whispered Jacinta presently. "What do you think?"

Lucia shook her head. "I don't know."

"We can find out after we get home," declared Francisco confidently. "Surely somebody went to the Cova on the thirteenth."

The children did not have long to wait for their curiosity to be satisfied. In just a few minutes a disgusted and angry mayor was depositing them at the gate of the parish priest's house in Fatima. "Find your own way home," he ordered harshly. "And never again cause an honest man so much trouble."

Even as they stared in silence, the mayor's car swung quickly about and headed back towards Ourem. For a moment the children stood gazing after it. Then their glances met, and immediately it was as though a weight had been lifted from their hearts.

"He's gone!" cried Lucia joyfully. "He won't hurt us any more."

"We can go home now," declared Jacinta, jumping up and down in excitement. "Oh, let's run all the way!"

Very soon there was a joyful reunion as the Marto and dos Santos families welcomed back their lost children. And amid the babble of excited tongues, the little shepherds learned what had taken place on the thirteenth of August. On that dreadful day more than fifteen thousand people had been on hand at the Cova da Iria for the expected apparition. Until noon they had been patient enough, reciting the Rosary and singing hymns. Then they had grown restless. Where were the children? they kept asking. Where was the lady? Then the news of the kidnapping burst like a bomb-shell.

"When some of the men heard about *that*, they wanted to go at once to Ourem and have things out with the mayor," said Manuel Marto, his hands clenching at the mere thought of what had been done to his little son and daughter.

"Don't forget that many people also thought Father Ferreira was connected in some way with the kidnapping," put in Lucia's father. "Quite a crowd went to his house from the Cova. Really angry they were, too, and no one knows what they might have done to him if they had found you children on his property."

Lucia clasped her hands. "And what did *you* think, Mother?"

Maria Rosa dos Santos smiled grimly. She loved her daughter, but hers was a stern nature and she still had scruples concerning the apparitions in the Cova. "I? Why, I thought as any sensible creature would think. I said to myself: 'If these children have been telling lies, here's their punishment. If they've been telling the truth, Our Lady will take care of them.' "

As time passed the whole story was told and retold, and the children began to understand why no one had gone to Ourem on the thirteenth to protest against the mayor's actions. True, the crowd in the Cova had been restless and disappointed—first, because of the children's absence, second, because they had been hoping to see a miracle and now they felt themselves cheated. But then something truly extraordinary had happened, and the whole atmosphere had changed.

"I guess your lady did come, although we didn't see her," said Jacinta's mother reverently. "Oh, children! I'll never forget the wonder as long as I live!"

The three little shepherds looked up eagerly. "What happened, Mother?" cried Francisco. "Please tell us!"

Olimpia Marto smiled. "Well, as the thousands of people in the Cova were arguing among themselves and wondering what to do, there was a sudden clap of thunder. It was a clear day, so this surprised everyone. Then there was a flash of lightning, so dazzling that it could be seen in spite of the sunshine. Then the sun began to grow pale, and a glowing cloud settled about the little holm-oak and hid it from view. Truly, I don't understand how it came there."

NO ONE HAD EVER SEEN SUCH A CLOUD.

"Neither does anyone else understand," added her husband. "Why, no one in Fatima ever saw a cloud like that—shining and radiant and just large enough to hide one holm-oak tree."

Lucia's father looked thoughtfully out of the window. "There's one thing certain," he remarked slowly. "Most of the people came to the Cova on the thirteenth hoping to see something out of the ordinary. When you children didn't arrive, they were deeply disappointed. They began to make fun of the lady and everything connected with her. They even made fun of you, too, and said it was a good thing the mayor of Ourem had taken you away."

"Yes, but it was a different matter when they saw the lightning and heard the thunder," put in Manuel Marto. "And when the cloud came and settled over the little tree—well, here was a heavenly sign that satisfied all of them. Believe me, there was no more scoffing or complaining then. In fact, there was more honest praying in the Cova on the thirteenth than ever before."

His wife nodded vigorously. "That's right. The crowd had been in rather bad spirits when they heard that you children would not be coming and that probably there would be no heavenly sign. Some had wanted to go to Ourem to protest against the mayor's action. Others insisted that he had done the right thing when he put you under arrest. But after the cloud came, all was peace."

For a moment Lucia was silent. Then she raised shining eyes to the grown-ups gathered about her. "Everyone believes in the lady now?" she asked hopefully. "They say the Rosary every day with real love?"

Her father smiled. "Most people believe, child. I think there will be more pilgrims than ever for the lady's September visit. But what a pity that she couldn't have come to you in August as she promised!"

Jacinta's eyes were solemn. "Yes, the lady was to have paid us six visits, but now I guess there'll be only five."

Francisco sighed. "We lost the August visit when we had to go to jail," he said, and there was real sorrow in his voice.

But it was not long before this sorrow was turned into an unexpected joy—for Lucia and Jacinta as well as for Francisco. The next day, August 19, while the three were pasturing their sheep some distance from home, near the village of Valinhos, there was a sudden and dazzling light in the branches of a small tree, then a burst of thunder. Turning, the three little shepherds saw the lady. As was her custom in the Cova da Iria, she was standing atop a tree, her feet hidden in a shimmering cloud, her garments of white and gold so bright that the children could barely manage to gaze upon her.

Lucia ran eagerly toward the vision. "Oh, thank you for coming!" she cried. "You know, we didn't think we'd see you until next month."

But even as she spoke, the little girl fell back a few paces. Why, something was wrong! The lady's face was pale and grave, just as though she were angry about something.

"What is it?" faltered the child. "Why do you look that way?"

For a moment all was silence. Then the lady began to speak in slow and measured tones. "I am very displeased with the mayor of Ourem," she declared. "He had no right to take you away from Fatima and to treat you so cruelly."

Lucia had forgotten all about the mayor, carried out of herself with delight at this surprise visit from her beloved friend. But now she listened anxiously as the lady repeated that she was deeply offended by the mayor's actions, that such sinful conduct must be punished and that all Portugal must share in the punishment.

"When I came to you children in July, I promised to tell you in October who I am and to work a great miracle then that would convince people that I am real," she said slowly. "But now, because of the mayor's actions, the miracle will be much less impressive than the one I had planned."

The sorrow in the lady's voice was so intense that it was some time before Lucia could find sufficient courage to ask a question that had been bothering many in Fatima, especially her mother. But finally words came—for this, and for one other question. For instance, what was to be done with the money that people were starting to leave in the Cova, beside the little holm-oak? Also would it be possible for the lady to bring back Manuel Marto (Jacinta's big brother) from the war soon? He was needed at home so very much!

"Use the money to buy two small stretchers to carry in processions," said the lady. "You and Jacinta will carry one of these stretchers, Lucia, with the help of two other little girls. Francisco and three of his friends will carry the second stretcher. All of you are to be dressed in white when you carry the stretchers to the parish church."

Lucia nodded, understanding full well what the lady meant. In small Portuguese villages such as Fatima, religious processions occurred many times during the year with every able-bodied person taking an active part. Generally there were groups of six to eight men in the procession, who carried large stretchers on their shoulders, supporting life-sized statues of saints. Preceding them were groups of children who carried small stretchers supporting small statues.

"What shall we carry on our stretchers?" asked Lucia.

The lady's eyes rested lovingly on the little girl before her. "Carry the offerings which people leave near the holm-oak. Use these offerings to promote devotion to Our Lady of the Rosary and also for the erection of a chapel in her honor."

"And Manuel Marto—you'll bring him home soon?"

The lady nodded. "Yes. All the troops will be brought home soon."

Presently, as on the occasions of her three other visits, the lady told the children to recite the Rosary devoutly each day and to make many sacrifices for sinners. Then she began to glide eastward from the top of the tree. In a moment she had disappeared into thin air, leaving the young shepherds gazing after her with rapt faces.

"Oh, how beautiful she is!" sighed Jacinta after a moment's silence. "Lucia, whenever the lady comes, I always feel so happy—even when she's gone away. Why, right now I feel I could walk on air!"

Her cousin nodded. "Yes. I know that feeling. And see that tree, Jacinta? The one where the lady stood? I'm going to break off a branch and take it home to Mother. Maybe when she sees it she'll feel as happy as we do."

ARIA ROSA dos Santos made little comment when the morning's great adventure was told to her. But she did admit that the branch which Lucia had brought home gave forth a wonderfully sweet fragrance. Friends and neighbors also bore witness to this, and soon everyone in Fatima had heard about the lady's visit at Valinhos.

"You knew all along that she was going to be there," said one old woman in a disappointed voice. "Oh, children! Why didn't you tell us? We could have gone to Valinhos, too."

"But we didn't know anything special was going to happen!" Lucia hastened to insist. "The lady's visit at Valinhos was truly a surprise."

"She'll be coming there next month, though, won't she?"

The little girl shook her head. "Oh, no! In September the lady will be at the Cova as usual."

As August passed and the thirteenth day of September approached, interest in the apparitions increased throughout all Portugal. Articles on the strange happenings in the Cova da Iria appeared in newspapers and magazines. Fatima, hitherto an almost unknown mountain village, became the most talked-about spot in the country. Devout men and women discussed ways and means of reaching it. Others, not so devout, asked one another if it would not be a good idea to go to this little village, some sixty miles north of Lisbon, and engage in a business there. Perhaps a hotel could be built or a shop opened.

"We ought to act quickly," they said. "Fatima may turn out to be a second Lourdes."

On May 13, when the lady had paid her first visit to the children, there had been no witnesses to the wonder. Ever since, however, many people had been on hand at the time of the expected visits. For instance, in June about seventy men and women had seen the lightning, heard the thunder, watched the three little shepherds as they gazed in awed delight upon their heavenly visitor. In July more than five thousand had come. In August (when the children were absent) some fifteen thousand people had been on hand. But in September! Why, all roads leading to Fatima were blocked with pilgrims! They came in wagons and on foot—at least thirty thousand of them eager to be present for the lady's fifth visit. Many hours before noon they had packed themselves into the Cova as best they could. The majority knelt and recited the Rosary, the men bare-headed as though in church, the women wearing the colorful veils of the Portuguese country districts. But when Lucia, Francisco and Jacinta arrived, the assembled people rose to their feet.

The children scarcely noticed the respect paid them—the whisperings, the admiring glances. Their minds were full of but one thought: *in a few minutes they would see their heavenly friend once more!* However, as they went toward the little holm-oak where they were accustomed to kneel and recite the Rosary while waiting for the lady, Lucia suddenly turned and faced the crowd.

"You must pray," she declared. "You must pray very hard."

The child's voice carried clearly, and at once there was a mighty rumbling. The thirty thousand people who had risen to greet the little shepherds were now falling to their knees. Hundreds were weeping, for few had come to the Cova out of idle curiosity. Many had brought hearts laden with grief, burdens which only the Queen of Heaven could lighten or remove. Now, how wonderful if it were really true that she was about to manifest herself to these three children of Fatima! If this were so, surely she loved them very much. Surely she planned to do great things for them, and for their friends who believed in her and who came on this and other pilgrimages to the Cova.

"Oh, I'm sure it's this way!" whispered a young woman from Lisbon to her husband. "Just look at those children's faces! They're not the faces of liars."

The man agreed, and began to finger his beads with more than usual devotion. But he had not finished even the first decade before real excitement broke out. The sun, a few seconds before a great fiery ball in the cloudless blue sky, had grown strangely dim. Indeed, before the astonished eyes of the thirty thousand people it had suddenly become little more than a pale yellow disc!

"They say this happens just before the lady appears to the children," explained the young wife in awed tones.

"She's so bright and beautiful that the sun becomes as nothing in her presence."

Before the husband could reply, a great shout went up throughout the Cova. "The lady! The lady! She's coming! Look over there!"

The young couple turned, then gasped. A small, shining cloud was gliding majestically across the sky from east to west. Slowly it moved earthwards, then settled about the little holm-oak. As it did so, the faces of the three children grew radiantly happy. And though the crowd could not see any vision, it felt confident that the lady had come to her young friends again. For the fifth time she was visible to them, standing atop the little tree, clothed in dazzling white and gold!

Half-realizing the wonder that was hidden from her own eyes, the young wife presently hazarded a guess as to what was happening. "I'm sure that the three children are seeing the lady now," she whispered. "The boy hears nothing of what is said; the smaller girl hears but does not speak. But the older girl—oh, just look at her! She's forgotten that thirty thousand people are watching her every action. She sees and hears no one but the lady!"

Yes, as on previous occasions, ten-year-old Lucia was beside herself with joy. Her heavenly friend had come again, and now nothing mattered but making the best possible use of the time of her visit.

"What do you want us to do?" she asked quickly.

The lady's eyes were grave. "Continue to say the Rosary every day, especially for the intention that the war may end soon."

"And the sick people here—are you going to cure them?"

"I shall cure some of them but not all, because the Lord places no trust in them. As for you, I want you to give me your word that you will be here without fail on the thirteenth day of next month. On that day I will not come to you alone, but in the company of Saint Joseph and the Child Jesus. Will you promise faithfully to be here?"

Lucia nodded eagerly. "Oh, yes! The three of us will be here at noontime."

The heavenly one seemed pleased with these words, but apparently she had no more to say. With a fond glance at the little shepherds, she began to glide from the top of the holm-oak into the air. Regretfully Lucia realized that the visit was over and turned toward the great crowd packed into the Cova.

"The lady's going away," she said.

Even as the child spoke, the white cloud lifted from about the holm-oak and rose slowly into the sky. Then it moved toward the east and disappeared. Almost at the same instant a shower of white petals began to rain down upon the children and the little oak tree.

"Look! Flowers from heaven!" cried hundreds with one voice.

"Yes! Catch them! Catch them!" came a second chorus.

But although there was a mad rush forward, no one succeeded in catching even one petal. Just a few feet above the ground the mysterious white flowers had suddenly melted away into thin air!

"Don't get excited," observed a well-dressed gentleman, obviously from the city. "That was only a trick arranged by the children's parents."

At this there was a horrified gasp from all sides. "A trick? Oh, no, sir! Don't say such things!"

"Why not? People often arrange affairs like this to get free publicity. I know. I'm in the newspaper business."

"LOOK! FLOWERS FROM HEAVEN!"

For a moment all was silence. Then an old shepherd stepped forward, his gnarled hand pointed warningly at the stranger. "Don't you know that Our Lady's been here?" he piped shrilly. "That God sent the white flowers to show us that the Cova is now a holy place?"

The newspaperman laughed. "Well, good friend, if Our Lady *has* been here, and if this *is* a holy place, why didn't the parish priest come today on the pilgrimage? I was hoping to see him and to ask him some questions, but they say he's not here."

The old man looked steadfastly at the newcomer, then lowered his eyes. "Father Ferreira's very busy," he muttered. "After all, there are many things to do in a country parish like Fatima."

"Oh, so he's really not here today?"

"No."

"But he's been here for the lady's other visits?"

"No. He's never come for any of the visits."

At this the stranger laughed loud and long. Then he nodded good-naturedly. "Well, thank you, my friend. I guess I've seen enough to know what everything's about. I'll get back to the city now and write my story."

But such a careless attitude caused the old shepherd to issue a second warning. "Don't make fun of what goes on here, sir. This is a holy place. And our good priest loves the Blessed Virgin as much as anyone."

"Then how do you explain that he doesn't come here to pray with his people? Isn't he interested in the lady? Doesn't he believe that the little ones see her?"

The old man hesitated. Then he made the Sign of the Cross, slowly and devoutly. "Our pastor is being careful," he said. "He knows that the enemies of the Church are waiting to criticize him even more than they have done."

CHAPTER NINE

It was true. From the beginning, the mayor of Ourem had insisted that there was nothing supernatural about the happenings in the Cova. Indeed, he continued to declare that the three little shepherds were conspirators in a scheme to make money for the parish church.

"One of these days they'll be charging admission to the Cova," he sneered. "Wait and see."

Father Ferreira believed that he could best deny such falsehoods by remaining away from the Cova on the days when the lady was expected. Of course he would have much preferred to be on hand with the others, since by now he was convinced that the three children really did experience a heavenly vision and that for some strange reason the Blessed Virgin had chosen them to do a special work for souls. However, until the Bishop was willing to declare himself in favor of the pilgrimages and devotions in the Cova, he felt that he should not make any move that might be misunderstood. And of course the Bishop could not form an opinion until many wise and holy priests had visited Fatima, questioned the children thoroughly, then returned with their reports and comments. All in all, reflected Father Ferreira, it might be several months before an official statement was forthcoming from the Bishop.

"And that's the way it ought to be," he told himself emphatically. "After all, we should be very prudent in this whole matter of the lady and her visits. We don't want to give our enemies a chance to laugh at us by calling something a miracle before we're sure."

There was not too long to wait, however, for a careful inquiry to begin. Two weeks after the lady's fifth visit—on September 27—a strange priest arrived at the dos Santos house. He was a professor of theology at the seminary in Lisbon, and he had come to question the three little shepherds as to the recent happenings in the Cova.

74

"I'd like to speak with Lucia first," he informed the child's mother. "Is she here?"

The latter, surprised and flustered in the midst of her housework, shook her head. No, Lucia was not at home. She was a mile away, picking grapes on a little piece of property belonging to the family. But of course someone could go for her ...

"That's all right," said the visitor kindly. "If Lucia isn't here just now, perhaps I could talk to Francisco and Jacinta. They live in the neighborhood, don't they?"

Maria Rosa nodded, hastily excused herself, then ran breathlessly to the house of her sister-in-law. For many weeks strangers had been stopping by and asking for permission to speak with Lucia and her cousins. Most of them were simple countryfolk who wanted to hear about the heavenly lady from the children's own lips. But now a priest had come—and a learned professor from the seminary at that! Why, with such visitors, surely the children would soon be considering themselves really important! And in a little while they would be well on the way to being completely spoiled.

"Holy Mother of God!" thought Marie Rosa frantically. "Why did I ever tell Lucia she might take the sheep to pasture? If I'd only kept her at home, there might never have been all this fuss about a heavenly lady in the Cova ... "

Chapter 10 The Great Miracle

POOR Maria Rosa! As the days passed, more and more strangers came to her house. By now it was understood that the learned priest from Lisbon had been much impressed with what had been told him by the three little shepherds, and finally there was scarcely an hour of the day when crowds of friends and strangers were not waiting to see them.

"Lucia, is it true that the lady is going to work a great miracle the next time she comes?" asked one woman eagerly.

"Tell me, Jacinta—is she really the Blessed Virgin?" put in another.

"What about the sick, Francisco?" cried a third. "Are there going to be cures in the Cova as there are at Lourdes?"

The three children answered the stream of questions in an unaffected and matter-of-fact manner. Yes, the lady was going to work a great miracle on the thirteenth day of October. And she was also going to say who she was, why she had come to the Cova, and what she wanted of the people gathered there. More wonderful still, this time she was going to bring with her two heavenly companions—Saint Joseph and the Child Jesus!

Naturally every newspaper in Portugal continued to be interested in the happenings at Fatima—especially in the children's prophecy that something of a miraculous nature would occur in the Cova on October 13. As the days passed, still more reporters and photographers were sent to the children's homes to interview them and to take their pictures. Unbelievers as well as devout men and women followed the Fatima story, and presently thousands of guesses were being made as to the nature of the great miracle.

"Don't you really know what it's going to be, Lucia?" asked Father Ferreira shortly before the important day.

The child shook her head. "No, Father. The lady didn't say. But in August she did tell us that it wouldn't be as great a wonder as she had planned at first. That's because she is still displeased over what the mayor of Ourem did to us."

The parish priest looked closely at the ten-year-old child before him. "Suppose nothing wonderful happens on the thirteenth. Aren't you afraid that people will laugh at you then?"

Lucia smiled. "No, Father."

"But they'll say you're a silly little girl! Think how bad your parents will feel over that!"

The child clasped her hands confidently. "Oh, Father, please don't worry! I *know* something wonderful is going to happen on the thirteenth! The lady told us so."

Repeated questionings could not change Lucia's mind on this score. Francisco and Jacinta were equally convinced that on October 13 there would be a great miracle to prove that the lady really came from heaven and that for some special reason God had permitted her to appear to them six times. And they were not surprised when they discovered on the day before the expected wonder that at least sixty thousand people had descended upon Fatima. Nor were they worried that these people talked openly of the miracle, and that they were prepared to spend the night in the sheep pasture in order to have a good view of the little holm-oak the next morning.

"In the end they'll be glad they came," the children told their families. "Wait and see."

The next morning dawned cold and rainy. By now the crowd had increased to seventy thousand persons, and Lucia's mother was beside herself with anxiety. What a disgrace for the family if the much-talked-of miracle did not occur! How angry and disappointed the great crowd of strangers would be who had spent a wet and chilly night in the Cova!

"The place must be nothing but a sea of mud by now," she thought, "and those poor people soaked to the skin. Oh, Lucia! Are you *very* sure that there is a heavenly lady?"

With tireless patience the child reassured her mother for still another time. Yes, there really was a heavenly lady. And in a little while she would work a miracle for everyone to see.

It was about half-past eleven when the youngsters and their families arrived at the sheep pasture. What a sight greeted their eyes! Huddled under dripping umbrellas were seventy thousand people—cold, muddy, tired. Behind them in an enormous jumble were the wagons, bicycles, automobiles and assorted beasts of burden which had brought them to the Cova. Rosaries were in every hand, and as the little ones appeared a thunderous murmur ran through the crowd. Even the unbelievers jerked to attention.

"Make way, everybody! The children are here!"

At once the vast throng fell back, and the three hurried toward the holm-oak, now little more than a bare trunk because so many devout men and women had carried home leaves and twigs as relics. Glancing briefly at the rain-soaked pilgrims, Lucia ordered that all umbrellas be closed and the Rosary recited by everyone present. Then, heedless of the chill rain and not at all flustered or self-conscious, she knelt upon the muddy ground to recite the same prayer with Francisco and Jacinta.

There in the cold downpour seventy thousand voices were now raised in honest supplication. People from all walks of life were present, each with some favor to ask the Queen of Heaven. But as noon came and went and the expected wonder did not take place, a feeling of uneasiness crept through the Cova. Perhaps the children had been mistaken! Perhaps the lady wasn't coming after all!

"Little fools! They've really tricked us this time!" cried one man, his patience at an end after nearly twenty-four hours of a wet and chilly vigil. "They said the lady would be here at noon. Well, where is she?"

The words had scarcely left his mouth when Lucia turned a radiant face to the great throng gathered about her. "She's coming! Kneel down, everybody!"

Maria Rosa, kneeling a few feet away, clasped her hands nervously. "Take a good look, child!" she cried. "Don't make any mistake!"

But Lucia was not making any mistake. How could she? An instant before the lady had truly come again, bright and beautiful in her white dress and her mantle edged in burnished gold. Right now she was standing above the barren

79

trunk of the little holm-oak—her eyes grave, her whole bearing that of a person with some deep and secret sorrow.

The crowd could not see the heavenly visitor, but the rapt look on the children's faces as well as the forcefulness in Lucia's voice were convincing proofs that something extraordinary was taking place. So, wet and cold, and with no place to kneel but in the mud, everyone obeyed Lucia's order. And as each heart beat expectantly, there were gasps of astonishment from all sides. A white cloud, seemingly of incense, was coming to rest about the tree! Three times the marvel was repeated, and then the cloud rose a few feet into the air and remained there, motionless. As this happened, the faces of the three children began to shine with an indescribable happiness.

"They must be seeing the lady," the devout onlookers told one another in awed voices. "And Lucia—yes, she seems to be speaking to her!"

It was true. The ten-year-old girl had always been the spokesman on the occasions of the lady's visits, and now she was losing no time in resuming her role. Looking directly at the heavenly visitor, she asked the first question—one which all Portugal was waiting to have answered.

"Who are you?"

The lady's face was grave. "I am the Lady of the Rosary."

"What do you want?"

"I have come to warn the faithful to change their lives and to ask pardon for their sins. They must not continue to offend Our Lord, already so deeply offended. And they must say the Rosary."

For a moment Lucia considered these words, her heart beating fast with excitement. So the beautiful one who had come to them six times was Our Lady of the Rosary! But before she had a chance for any real reflection, the familiar and beautiful voice was sounding once more:

"I wish to have a chapel built here in my honor as the Lady of the Rosary. And this is the message I promised to bring, Lucia. Tell the people that I will answer their prayers and cause the war to end soon if they will change their lives."

The little girl listened carefully, promising to do her best to pass along the new message to others. Then she looked hesitantly at her heavenly friend. Perhaps now it would be all right to state the various petitions given to her beforehand by anxious friends and neighbors?

The lady seemed to understand the unspoken plea and to consent to it as well, and so immediately Lucia began her questioning. For instance, would a certain poor woman recover her health? Would another woman live to see her son return from the war? Would this family have a plentiful harvest? Would that family sell their farm at a good price?

The lady's replies were brief and to the point. Certain of the petitions would be granted, others refused. And as she looked upon the children, the heavenly one let each understand that this was her last visit with them in the Cova. Yes, she was the Blessed Virgin, and now she had finished the work given her to do by her Divine Son. She had instilled in the hearts of three little shepherds a knowledge of the wonderful power of the Rosary to win graces for souls, as well as a deep love for it. But this knowledge and this love were not to be kept locked in the hearts of her little friends. No, indeed. They were to be handed on to others, for it was God's Will that loyal Catholics everywhere should know and love this wonderful prayer—should recite it each day, reverently and willingly. If they did so, what splendid graces the Lady of the Rosary would pour out upon them!

What untold sorrows would she turn away from their homes!

Presently the children realized that the lady was about to leave them. As usual she was gliding eastwards from above the holm-oak into thin air. But just before she disappeared from view, she raised her hand and pointed to the sun. Not realizing what she did, Lucia excitedly repeated the gesture.

"Look at the sun!" she cried to those kneeling about her.

As the clear, young voice rang through the Cova, all eyes turned heavenwards. Why, wonder of wonders! The rain was over and the sun, hidden for hours by ominous clouds, was now shining in a clear blue sky! But not in its usual form of a dazzling fiery ball. No, this time it resembled a dull silver disc at which anyone could gaze without eyestrain.

A white-haired farmer turned anxiously to his wife. "In all my eighty years I never saw the sun look like that," he faltered. "If my eyes are getting bad again . . ."

The latter stretched forth a comforting hand. "No, no! It's the miracle that the children promised. Don't you remember?"

Reassured, the old man nodded slowly—not realizing that in one sense his good wife was mistaken. For this was not the entire miracle, only the beginning of it, and even as the woman was attempting to refresh her husband's memory concerning the children's prophecy, the second part began. Impelled by some mysterious force, suddenly the dull silver disc that was the sun began to whirl in the sky. It was like an unearthly wheel revolving at terrific speed, casting off great shafts of colored light with every turn. Green, red, blue, violet, yellow—the enormous rays shot across the sky at all angles, lighting up the entire countryside but particularly the Cova, where seventy thousand people stood spellbound, their uplifted faces blank with astonishment at this spectacle of a silver sun revolving in a myriad of colored rays.

The wonder lasted three minutes, after which the sun ceased its whirling and the shafts of light disappeared. But just as the crowd was catching its breath and prepared to discuss the marvel, it began again—for a second, then a third time. Soon it seemed that the whole world was on fire, for by now the colored shafts were like flaming swords that slashed across the sky, the mountains, the sheep pasture, the upturned faces of the people—crossing, re-crossing, with never a moment's rest. The sun was also revolving at an even more intense speed. Then suddenly there was a great gasp of terror. *It seemed as though the dull silver disc in the sky was tearing itself from the heavens and was about to crash down upon the mass of people packed together in the Cova!*

"It's the end of the world!" cried one woman hysterically.

"Dear God, don't let me die in my sins!" shrieked another.

"Holy Virgin, protect us!" implored a third.

For twelve minutes everyone in the Cova forgot about the three little shepherds, the heavenly lady, the prophecy that something wonderful would take place on October 13. Instead, they were concerned with making Acts of Contrition, with beating their breasts over long-cherished sins, with weeping and groaning. Forgotten also was the muddy sheep pasture, trampled for hours by thousands of feet. Now there was the spectacle of fashionably-dressed men and women from the city kneeling in the mud, tears streaming down their terrified faces, every nerve and muscle tense with dread.

Then, as quickly as it had begun, the wonder came to an end. The sun turned from pale silver to bright gold, and the shafts of colored light faded from the sky. All was normal once more. But as one person looked at another—still shaking, still not sure that the end of the world was not about to occur—there were expressions of astonishment on all sides. Garments soaked by hours of rain had dried perfectly during the course of the twelve minute wonder! And despite the fact that everyone had been kneeling in the mud, both the clothes and their wearers were now free from stain!

"It's another part of the great miracle!" cried someone. "The lady is truly the Blessed Mother to have such care of us!"

"Yes, and there's been a cure, too," called out a second voice. "A woman over here was dying and now she's quite well."

At this, fresh excitement broke forth from all sides. A cure! Oh, how good God was! And His Blessed Mother! But if the people were amazed at these signs just given them to prove that the heavenly lady was real, their amazement knew no bounds when they discovered that the three little shepherds had experienced additional marvels. While the sun had been whirling in the heavens, they had enjoyed a beautiful vision of the Holy Family.

Yes, and there had been even more for Lucia. To her Our Lord had appeared as a grown man dressed in red, accompanied by His Mother, the Lady of Sorrows. Then Our Lady had shown herself to Lucia again—although not garbed as before, or in the garments of dazzling white and gold which she had worn on her other visits in the Cova. No, this time she was dressed in a brown religious habit and held in her hand a scapular of Mount Carmel. And contrary to Lucia's experience in the previous apparitions, none of the figures in the latest visions had spoken to her.

THEY HAD ENJOYED A VISION OF THE HOLY FAMILY.

"Where did you see these wonderful things, child?" asked a man's reverent voice suddenly. "Over the holm-oak?" The little girl shook her head. "No, sir. Up in the sky— at one side of the sun as it was whirling about."

At this Jacinta turned a puzzled face to her brother. "But I saw only one picture," she whispered, "the one of the Holy Family. Did you see any others, Francisco?"

The latter was almost in a trance, and at first did not hear the question. Then very slowly he came to himself. No, he had seen only the Blessed Mother, in a white dress with a blue mantle, accompanied by Saint Joseph and the Child Jesus, both in red garments.

"The Child Jesus was about a year old, and He was nestling in Saint Joseph's arms," the little boy murmured dreamily, his shining eyes blind to the crowd that pressed about on all sides. "Oh, and He was beautiful, Jacinta! So beautiful . . ."

LL FATIMA was swept out of every appearance of normalcy by the miracle, and for the rest of the day there were nothing but demands to see and speak with the children. Maria do Carmo, the woman who had been cured, was also surrounded by eager questioners, and she willingly told what she could—of herself, her illness, her twenty-two mile barefoot pilgrimages from Maceira to the Cova, of which this trip today was the third.

"Last July I was dying of tuberculosis," she explained to those who pressed about her. "When I heard about the visits of the heavenly lady here, I promised to make four pilgrimages, barefoot, to obtain my cure."

At this a murmur of astonishment ran through the crowd. Four barefoot pilgrimages of forty-four miles each, over stony roads and steep hills! What a spirit of sacrifice was here!

"The first trip in August was very hard," the woman continued. "My husband and I set out at one o'clock in the morning and he was almost sure that I would die on the road. But I dragged myself along, just one big pain from head to foot."

"Ah, but didn't you forget all the suffering when you finally reached here?" asked a thin-faced woman, obviously afflicted with the same ailment which Maria do Carmo had known for five years.

The latter nodded eagerly. "Yes, just a few minutes after arriving I felt much better. Of course the lady didn't come here in August—since the children were in prison at Ourem —but she helped me just the same. I did not suffer so much on the trip back home."

"And you walked those twenty-two miles again in September? And barefoot both ways?"

"Yes. And without too much difficulty. But today—oh, thanks be to the Holy Mother—I feel as though I could run all the way home!"

"You stood for hours in the rain here this morning, too, didn't you, before the lady came?"

"Yes. And like the others I was cold and soaked to the skin. The pain was bad, too. But now look at me! My cough is gone. The swelling has left my arms and legs. I have no pain anywhere. Oh, truly this Cova is a holy place!"

Before twenty-four hours had passed, the story of Maria do Carmo's cure, but more especially that of the sun's mysterious whirling, had spread throughout all Portugal. The photographers who had been present in the Cova had taken pictures of the "dancing sun," and now these appeared in every newspaper. There were the giant rays shooting forth, the uplifted faces of the pilgrims—each with its expression of astonishment, wonder, fear. There were the children kneeling by the holm-oak, carried out of themselves at the beauty of their heavenly friend. Truly, the stupendous wonder of October 13 had been well recorded by the cameras.

But everyone was not convinced. Within a few days after the miracle, a group of atheists crept into the Cova by night and destroyed a wooden arch which devout pilgrims had erected over the place of the apparitions. They also overturned a table whereon the faithful were accustomed to leave their offerings, stole the lamps burning there and other pious objects as well. Then they cut down what they thought to be the holm-oak upon which Our Lady's feet had rested.

Fortunately the atheists overlooked the real tree (now little more than a root in the ground), but in a spirit of malice the tree they did choose was tied to the back of their automobile and dragged over the dusty road to the neighboring town of Santarem. Here, on October 25, it was paraded through the streets, together with the other pious objects stolen from the Cova, while hundreds jeered and mocked at the mere mention of the heavenly lady, the three little shepherds, the Catholic faith.

"Who wants to be led astray by superstitious peasants from Fatima?" cried these unbelievers. "Let's be wise like the political leaders in Russia. This very month they've discovered what the priests have been trying to keep from them for centuries: that there is no God or a life after death!"

Yes, it was October, 1917, and atheistic Communism had been unleashed upon Russia and the world. Once again the Devil was making use of certain wicked men in an effort to snatch souls to himself, to keep them from occupying the places in heaven which he and his angels had forfeited so long ago.

"Perhaps that's why the Blessed Virgin came to the Cova," certain people told themselves. "She wants to defeat the Devil, and she knows that the Rosary is one of the most powerful weapons against him."

"If that's true, we ought to learn whatever Fatima has to teach us about saying the Rosary daily with real care and devotion," said others. "Then maybe the Devil's campaign in Russia will fail, and there'll be a chance to have real peace in the world."

"Yes," agreed still more people. "The Devil is behind most of the world's troubles. Despite appearances, it is he who sets different classes and nations against one another."

The three little shepherds never guessed that these and similar conversations were taking place throughout all Portugal, that suddenly thousands of men and women had taken to saying the Rosary every day, that Lucia's account of the lady's visits was appearing in dozens of newspapers. No, after the sixth apparition in the Cova, just as after the first, the children remained simple and unspoiled. Not even the crowds which continued to come on pilgrimages to Fatima could make them consider themselves important. Indeed, in one sense Lucia had small chance to become conceited, since her family still misunderstood and criticized her.

"The Cova used to be a good place to grow vegetables," grumbled her brother Manuel one day. "We could even get feed there for the mules. Now every blade of grass has been trampled by the pilgrims. Not a thing is left growing. What are you going to do about that, little holy one?"

"Yes, and there's absolutely no peace for me any more," complained the oldest sister Therese. "People are always asking for Lucia. Then I have to leave my housework, try to remember where she is pasturing the sheep, and send someone to bring her home."

"What about us?" put in the other sisters, Gloria and Caroline. "Many times we have to take Lucia's place and watch the sheep while she sits chatting in the parlor with all kinds of important people. Oh, it really isn't fair!"

Their mother sighed. "I know that watching sheep is no work for big girls who know how to cook and spin and weave," she admitted. "It's for a little girl like Lucia who doesn't know anything. But what can I do? These days everyone is asking for her . . ."

Manuel shook his head gloomily. "I know what's going to happen," he declared. "We're going to have to sell the sheep."

Maria Rosa gasped. "*Sell the sheep?* But we get our wool from them! And meat! Why, we save a good deal of money because of those animals . . ."

"I know, Mother. But mark my words. Unless heaven works a miracle for *us,* and keeps people from wanting to see Lucia, the sheep will have to be sold. Really, sometimes I wonder why the lady didn't appear to a child whose family could afford the honor . . ."

Poor Lucia! It was hard to bear the cutting remarks of her good but misunderstanding relatives, and she often found herself in tears. At such times she would marvel at Jacinta's disappointment that Francisco and she were not also nagged and scolded by their family.

"If we were, think how many extra sacrifices we'd have to offer for sinners!" sighed the little girl one day. "Oh, Lucia, you *are* lucky . . ."

Francisco nodded. "Yes. And do you know something? I've found out that suffering isn't hard if you ask Our Lady to help you to bear it as Our Lord bore His—for the love of souls. It's only hard when you try to run away from it."

Jacinta's dark eyes lit up with a strange glow. "I've found that out, too," she said. "That's why I try to suffer a little something every day for souls. Only sometimes I know I could do a lot more, particularly when people are nice to me and everything goes well at home. Then I feel as though I ought to go out and find some suffering."

Lucia squirmed uneasily. "Jacinta, you're always talking about suffering for souls! But other people don't concern themselves with it. Why, they try to have things easy all the time!"

Now the light in Jacinta's eyes fairly sparkled. "*Other people?* But they never had a glimpse of hell as we did, Lucia. Oh, don't you remember that day in July when the lady showed us the billions and billions of damned souls in hell?"

Recalling the dreadful vision, and how all three of them had nearly died from terror, the older girl shivered. "Of course I remember! Who could ever forget how awful it was?"

Jacinta clasped her hands fervently. "It's too late to help those souls, but we can help others and keep them from going to hell. We can do it by suffering as the lady told us. Shall we try very hard to do that?"

"Oh, yes!" cried Francisco eagerly. "Let's pray and suffer as much as we can. That will surely save many souls and please the lady."

Naturally Lucia agreed to take part in this heavenly work, consoled by the thought that Francisco was right. Suffering for others could be a joyful matter if one remembered to ask the Blessed Virgin for a share in the love her Son bore for sinners, likewise for strength and courage to persevere in their salvation.

"I'll ask for this favor every day," the little girl thought. "I'm sure Our Lady always hears this kind of prayer."

THEY FREQUENTLY GAVE AWAY THEIR LUNCHES.

93

So it was that neither Lucia nor Francisco objected when Jacinta set herself to finding still more ways whereby the three of them could do penance for sinners. She had been the leader in this venture since the lady's visit in July, but because there had never been anyone to give advice on the subject, the mortifications she had chosen were inclined to be extreme. For instance, already she and her two play-mates had formed the habit of not drinking any water on certain days while watching the sheep—no matter how intense the heat. Again, they frequently gave away their lunches to some poor children in the neighborhood, contenting themselves with the bitter herbs and acorns they found in the fields. Or, if they did not give away their lunches to the poor children, they gave them to the sheep.

As a result of such rigorous fasting, the little ones frequently suffered from severe headaches during the long hours away from home. But spurred on by a holy desire to be victims for sinners, they bore the discomfort bravely. However, their heroism reached even greater heights when Lucia discovered a piece of rough rope along the highway.

"We'll cut this rope into three parts and each wear a piece about our waists," they decided. "Probably it will hurt after a while. Then we'll have another pain to offer up for sinners."

But the new penance was more difficult than the children had anticipated. Many days Jacinta could hardly keep back the tears because of the suffering it caused.

"Take off the rope," advised Lucia finally. "You'll make yourself sick if you keep on wearing it."

But the seven-year-old child shook her head. "What about the sinners? The only way to save them is by prayer and sacrifice, isn't it?"

So the weeks passed, and the children entered more deeply into the work of praying and suffering for others. Upheld by grace, which constantly flooded their hearts because they did not forget to ask the Blessed Mother for courage to do all that God desired of them, they became true victim souls. But no one, not even Father Ferreira, realized the wonderful fact.

"You don't suppose we should tell anyone how we are praying and suffering for sinners, do you?" asked Jacinta one day.

Francisco shook his head. "Oh, no! They wouldn't understand."

"Mother would say I was crazy," sighed Lucia. "I just know she would."

So the penitential side of their lives was kept a secret, and to all appearances the children were just as they had been before the lady's first visit. Each morning they took their parents' sheep to pasture—the usual task for young children in Portugal's country districts. On Sundays and feast days they accompanied their families to Mass in the village church, where occasionally Lucia was permitted to receive Holy Communion. But Francisco and Jacinta, not having reached the age of ten, were considered too young for the great honor. And of course they had never told anyone of the visits from the Angel of Peace, or of the wonderful day when he had permitted them to receive the Holy Eucharist in a miraculous fashion.

"Even if the Blessed Virgin did appear to the children, they still don't know all the Catechism," said their good mother placidly. "It wouldn't be right to let them receive Holy Communion yet."

But the little ones, instructed by Our Lady of the Rosary, knew far more about spiritual matters than anyone suspected. Indeed, from time to time there were discussions in the sheep pasture which would have astonished and alarmed their families.

"Lucia, didn't the lady tell you on the second visit that she was going to take Francisco and me to heaven soon?" asked Jacinta one day.

The latter hesitated. "Yes, she did say that."

"Well, I wonder what she means by 'soon'?"

Lucia shivered. "I don't know. Let's not talk about it."

"You mean, you're still sad because the lady said you couldn't go to heaven when we do?'

"That's right. She said I'd have to stay here in the world for some time yet. Oh, how can I live without you and Francisco?"

Jacinta's eyes were full of sympathy. "But the lady said she had work for you to do—that you're to help establish devotion to her Immaculate Heart! Oh, Lucia, that's really wonderful—to help other people to know and love the Immaculate Heart of Mary!"

Francisco nodded. "It's the finest work in the world. And we'll help you all we can up in heaven. Won't we, Jacinta?"

"Of course we will. But I still wonder . . . "

"You wonder what?"

"When we're going to go there."

Suddenly Lucia could bear such talk no longer. "You're going to go to school before you go to heaven," she said abruptly. "And so am I. I heard our parents talking about it just yesterday."

The eyes of Francisco and Jacinta grew round with surprise. "*School?* But why?"

"So you can learn to read and write."

"But what good is that if we're going to die soon?"

Francisco nodded vigorously. "It was *you* the lady said should learn to read, Lucia—not us. Don't you remember? She said that on her second visit in June."

With difficulty Lucia overcame a desire to burst into tears. Here truly was a double sacrifice to offer for sinners! First, her beloved cousins were going to die and leave her alone. Second, there were to be no more carefree hours in the fields —watching the sheep, playing games, reciting the Rosary. Instead, the future was to be devoted to lessons in a stuffy classroom, surrounded by strangers who at first would stare and whisper, then gain courage and ask endless questions about the heavenly lady.

Jacinta seemed to read her cousin's thoughts. "Let's say the prayer," she suggested.

So the three began the familiar and comforting words which the lady had taught them on her third visit in July: *"Oh, my Jesus, I offer this for the love of Thee, for the conversion of sinners, and in reparation for all the wrongs done to the Immaculate Heart of Mary."*

Even as she prayed, much of the burden lifted from Lucia's heart. Yes, it was going to be very hard to have to go to school, to be deprived in the near future of the companionship of Francisco and Jacinta. But if this was what God wanted—if the suffering would be of help to poor sinners . . .

"I feel much better now," she announced suddenly. "That prayer always helps."

FEW weeks after the great miracle, the three little shepherds began to attend school. As Lucia had foreseen, both students and teachers were consumed with curiosity, and not a day passed that she and her cousins did not have real sacrifices to offer for souls because of the many idle questions put to them.

"Why do the other children stare at us so?" asked Jacinta one day. "It's as though they thought something were wrong with us."

"Yes, and they get together and whisper things about the lady," added Francisco sadly, "things that aren't true. I've heard them. Oh, Lucia! I don't like school at all. Why do we have to go?"

The latter tried to hide her true feelings. "We have to go to school so that our parents won't have visitors in the house

98

all day asking for us. And so you two can prepare for your First Communion."

At this some of the sadness vanished from Jacinta's face. "That's right," she admitted. "We're learning the Catechism at school. And if we hurry up and finish the book, maybe they'll let us make our First Communion before we're ten years old."

Pondering this possibility, Francisco also was comforted. "I never thought of that," he said. "Oh, how wonderful that would be!"

"There's another thing," put in Lucia quickly. "Now that we come to the village every day for school, we have a chance to make visits to the Blessed Sacrament. We couldn't do that when we were taking care of the sheep."

The brother and sister looked at each other solemnly. How truly Lucia spoke! Why, before they had started coming to school, their only trips to the village church had been on Sundays and feast days to attend Mass. Now, despite the various people waiting at the church to see and speak with them, there was time to make one or more visits to the Blessed Sacrament every day!

"We mustn't complain about school any more," decided Jacinta finally. "Of course it's hard to be stared at and whispered about, but then the lady did ask if we'd be willing to help souls by suffering for them and we said we would."

"And she promised that God would help us to bear the suffering," added Lucia. "I often think of that when things get hard."

Francisco nodded. "That's why it's so nice to be able to go to church often," he said slowly. "Somehow, before the Tabernacle it seems much easier to ask God for His help."

So the months passed, and life for the children rolled on in orderly fashion. By the fall of 1918, the two girls had made excellent progress in their studies. But it was a different story with Francisco, for he had never been able to grow interested in school work. Realizing this, his teachers occasionally allowed him to stay away from class for a day or so, believing that a short rest would help him. But although the boy was pleased to have such free time, he knew that his teachers were mistaken. He would never achieve a real interest in reading or writing or arithmetic. After all, why should he? Hadn't the lady promised that very soon she would come and take him to heaven?

"Call for me at the church when school is over," he told Lucia and Jacinta on the occasions of his various holidays. "I'm going to say many Rosaries today."

The two girls were not at all surprised at these words, although eighteen months ago they would have been dumbfounded. For previous to the lady's first visit in the Cova, Francisco had been little interested in spiritual matters. Like many men and boys, he had believed that visits to the Blessed Sacrament, frequent reception of the Sacraments, the daily recitation of the Rosary, were meant only for women and girls. But what a difference since the Blessed Virgin had shown herself to him six times! Now he realized that each man and boy in the world, even as each woman and girl, has but one reason for existence: to know, love and serve God in this world by prayer and good works, then to be happy with Him forever in the next.

Yes, Francisco had learned a great deal since the lady's first visit in the Cova on May 13, 1917. Often he reminded himself of what she had said then: that soon she would take Jacinta and him to heaven, leaving Lucia on earth for an indefinite period.

"But she also said that I must say many Rosaries before she takes me to heaven, and say them properly," he thought. "Oh, I must get busy!"

So not a day passed that Francisco did not offer at least one-third of the Rosary—or five decades—to the Queen of Heaven. And for him, saying the Rosary was no longer a tiresome matter of repeating so many times the Our Father, Hail Mary and *Gloria*. No, now it was like looking at five, ten or fifteen beautiful pictures of Our Lord and the Blessed Virgin.

"The different pictures are the different mysteries of the Rosary," he told himself. "Oh, until the lady came, I never knew anything about them!"

So, even as Lucia and Jacinta, Francisco now recited the Rosary "properly" every day—that is, he chose a set of five pictures or events from the life of Our Lord or the life of the Blessed Virgin, either the Joyful, Sorrowful or Glorious mysteries, and looked upon each separately with the eyes of his soul. He did this while reciting the five decades of the Rosary. In other words, he meditated.

The practice was not too hard—even for a boy of ten years, such as Francisco, or a little girl of eight, such as Jacinta. Indeed, the three children rapidly became experts at calling to mind one or all fifteen of the mysteries of the Rosary. Thus, when offering the Joyful Mysteries, they knew that there were five pictures—or events in the life of Our Lord and the life of the Blessed Virgin—to look at. First, the Annunciation, when the Angel Gabriel came to the Blessed Virgin and told her that she was to be the Mother of God. Second, the Visitation, when the Blessed Virgin set out to visit her aged cousin Elizabeth. Third, the Nativity, or the Birth of Our Lord in Bethlehem. Fourth, the Presentation, when the Christ Child was brought to the Temple forty days after His birth and offered to God. Fifth, the Finding of the Child Jesus in the Temple by the Blessed Virgin and Saint Joseph.

It was the same when offering the Sorrowful Mysteries and the Glorious Mysteries. Once more there were groups of five pictures to consider—with sad scenes, happy scenes. Oh, truly, saying the Rosary properly was a splendid way to pray! Thus anyone, even small children, could win graces for souls who otherwise would go to hell because of their sins. And thus anyone could help put a stop to the war and bring lasting peace to the world. The heavenly lady—who was no other than the Mother of God—had said so!

The days passed, and more and more people became interested in saying the Rosary properly because of the wonderful events which had taken place at Fatima. Plans were even made to erect a little chapel in the Cova, since the lady had asked that this be done. But in the late fall of 1918, a terrible plague began sweeping over Europe which caused such plans to be suspended. Germany, France. Spain, Portugal—the dreaded influenza germ was striking everywhere. Overnight strong men fell victim to it, and in village and city the funeral bells tolled in constant requiem. Finally the awful malady reached Fatima, and among the first victims were the Marto and dos Santos families. Of these, Jacinta and Francisco were the most seriously afflicted.

The latter fell ill around Christmas time, and remained in a critical state for about two weeks. Then he began to improve. But when friends and family rejoiced at this, the little boy only shook his head weakly.

"I'm never going to be well again. I'm going to die."

"Nonsense!" cried his godmother. "I've made a promise to the Blessed Virgin, Francisco. If she cures you, I'm going to sell a quantity of my best wheat weighing as much as you do, and give the money toward building a chapel in her honor in the Cova."

Again the little boy shook his head. "You won't have to keep that promise, godmother. I know it."

The entire Marto family were perplexed and fearful because of Francisco's words. But Jacinta, recovering from the dread influenza in another room, felt that she understood what her brother meant. After all, the lady had said that she would take him to heaven soon. Well, perhaps "soon" had arrived! And so, when not saying the Rosary, the little girl frequently speculated as to what had happened and was going to happen to her beloved brother.

"Maybe the lady came and told him when she's going to take him to heaven," she thought. "Maybe she said when she was going to take me, too. Oh, how I wish I knew!"

But the lady had not appeared to Francisco yet. Then a few days later she did come. The unexpected apparition took place in the home of the two invalids, at a time when no one was about. Yes, it was God's Will that the Lady of the Rosary, radiant and lovely as on her previous visits, should make herself visible to her young friends for still another time. And as they looked upon her, garbed in her customary white and gold, the hearts of the little shepherds filled once more with unearthly joy. How beautiful the Blessed Virgin was! How kind and motherly! Why, one could spend an eternity looking at her and never grow tired.

Had Our Lady come to take them to heaven? Would they both die at once? Oh, surely so, for it would be very easy to give themselves into her keeping and go to see the saints ... the angels ... GOD! At least Francisco's death could not be very far away ... he had been sick for so many weeks ... Jacinta, too—she had suffered a great deal ...

Reading the children's jumbled thoughts like an open book, the lady smiled. "Not yet, Francisco," she said gently, "although in a very little while I shall come and take you to heaven as I promised. And as for you, Jacinta—are you willing to keep on suffering and convert still more sinners?"

THE THREE HAD A LITTLE VISIT IN FRANCISCO'S ROOM.

The little girl had ardently longed to go to heaven with Francisco, but at the sound of the lady's voice she was filled with wisdom beyond her years. In all things, it is best to have no will but the Will of God, to desire nothing but what will please Him most and help souls to merit His choicest gifts. Now, strengthened with this wonderful grace, she clasped her hands eagerly and looked up at the lady.

"I'll keep on suffering as long as God wishes! I'll save as many souls as I can!"

The lady smiled understandingly. "Then you will suffer much. You will even go to a hospital. But you will bear everything for the conversion of sinners, in reparation for offenses against the Immaculate Heart of Mary, and for the love of Jesus."

As she spoke these prophetic words, the heavenly one looked kindly at both children, then slowly faded from sight. Her latest visit to Fatima was over!

Naturally the brother and sister could hardly wait to share their wonderful news with Lucia. Francisco was going to die very soon, but Jacinta—convalescing from the influenza and able to walk again—was going to remain on earth somewhat longer. She was going to suffer still more for souls.

"I was right all along," Francisco confided when the opportunity came and Lucia, returning one afternoon from school, was permitted to visit briefly with Jacinta and himself. "I'm not going to get better, even if godmother did promise the Blessed Virgin that she would sell some of her best wheat and give the money toward building a chapel in the Cova."

Lucia's eyes were uneasy. "I guess the lady thinks you've said enough Rosaries," she observed, her heart torn for still another time as she looked on Francisco's wasted body and realized that the prophecy made so long ago in the sheep pasture was about to be fulfilled. "And I guess she thinks you've suffered enough, too."

"Yes. But there's one thing that troubles me."

"What?"

"I haven't made my First Communion like other children, at the church. Oh, Lucia! I never finished the Catechism at school. And now maybe they won't let me receive Our Lord . . ."

There was real longing in the boy's voice. But he offered his fear that he might die without having received Holy Communion as a sacrifice and said no more about it.

Now Easter was approaching, and the parish priest was eager that as many as possible of his people should approach the Sacraments for the great feast. He thought of little Francisco Marto, hesitating because the child had not finished the Catechism. Well, he was a good boy. Even if he had not finished the Catechism, surely he knew enough to understand what was meant by the Sacraments of Penance and Holy Eucharist? Surely he could make his Easter duty like others in the parish and thus share more fully in the numerous blessings of the holy season?

"I'll go and hear the lad's confession," the good priest decided. "And I'll bring him Holy Communion, too."

How happy Francisco was when he learned that his two great desires were about to be fulfilled! "You'll have to help me to examine my conscience," he told Lucia. "I want to have my soul really clean when Our Lord comes into it."

So the little girl did her best to aid her cousin in calling to mind his sins. For instance, in the past he had frequently disobeyed his mother. Did he remember all the times he had run out of the house when she had told him to stay inside?

And all the times when he had pretended not to hear her calling him?

Francisco nodded sorrowfully. "I remember. But what else have I done?"

Lucia shook her head. "I can't think of anything else. But maybe Jacinta can. After all, she lives with you."

So Jacinta came into the sick room, and after due thought she reminded her brother that before the lady's first visit he had taken ten cents from his father's purse without permission in order to buy a harmonica. And that when certain boys in Fatima had thrown stones at other boys from the neighboring town of Boleiros, he had thrown some, too.

Again Francisco nodded. "I remember. And I'm sorry. But what else have I done, Jacinta?"

His sister could think of no other sins. "Just tell the priest when he comes that you're sorry for these things and anything else you did that may have offended Our Lord. That's all that's necessary for a good Confession."

So on April 2, a few days before Easter, Francisco received the Sacrament of Penance, and early the next morning the pastor brought him Holy Communion. Later in the day, when Lucia and Jacinta crept into his room, they marveled at the new radiance upon his face.

"Francisco, aren't you suffering any more?"

"No, the pain has gone."

"Do you suppose the lady is coming today to take you to heaven?"

"I don't know. Nothing matters, now that I've been to Holy Communion."

Jacinta clasped her hands fervently. "Oh, it must be wonderful to receive Our Lord!"

"Wonderful? Oh, yes!"

"When you go to heaven, please greet Our Lord and Our Lady for me. Tell them that I'll suffer for sinners as much as they wish, and in reparation to the Immaculate Heart of Mary."

"I'll tell them."

Lucia knelt down by the bed. "Francisco, you will pray for us up in heaven?"

"Of course I'll pray! I'll ask Our Lord to let you and Jacinta come there real soon. But you ... you'll have to offer the Rosary for me today. I'm so tired ... "

The two girls promised to do this, then slowly took their leave. Would they ever speak with Francisco again? Would he live through this day—April 3? Surely not. But even as they shut the door to the sick room and stood looking at each other gravely in the hall outside, the bell in the distant church tower began to toll—slowly, solemnly.

Quickly Jacinta looked up, made the Sign of the Cross, then joined her hands in prayer. "The influenza—someone else has died of it!" she whispered. "Oh, Lucia! The next time the bells toll like this ... "

The latter nodded, her face pale and tense with grief. The next time the bells tolled like this it would mean that a little boy had gone to heaven.

Chapter 13 The Great Sacrifice

T WAS about six o'clock the next morning when Francisco suddenly stirred from a fitful sleep, raised himself in bed and pointed toward the door. His eyes were shining.

"Oh, Mother! Look at the beautiful light!"

At once Olimpia Marto was at her son's side. "I don't see any light, Francisco. Where is it?"

The youngster pointed again. "See? Near the door. Oh, how beautiful it is ... "

Olimpia looked once more, but saw nothing unusual. Then a moment later the boy gave a deep sigh and settled back on his pillow. "The light's gone, Mother. I don't see it now."

Believing that her little son was about to fall into a healthful slumber, Olimpia smiled understandingly, gave

109

him an affectionate pat, and slipped from the room. As she did so, Francisco's godmother entered. Seeing her, the boy stretched out his hands.

"I'm sorry for all the bad things I ever did," he murmured. "Really and truly, godmother."

The latter nodded kindly and came over to sit beside the bed. "Try to rest now," she whispered. "That's the only way to become strong and well."

But even as she spoke, something in the child's face caused the good woman to lean forward anxiously. Of a sudden her little godson seemed so peaceful ... so happy ... so *still!* Surely it couldn't be ...

"*Olimpia!*" she cried. "Olimpia, come here!"

At once Francisco's mother came running, but it was too late. Her youngest boy was just breathing his last. And without a doubt he was seeing something truly beautiful as he gave up his soul to God, for the smile upon his lips was not of this world.

Tears streaming down her face, Olimpia threw herself upon her knees beside the bed and for several minutes gave free vent to her grief. Francisco had died! On April 4, 1919, two months short of his eleventh birthday, he had gone home to God! But as her husband and other children came hurrying into the room, their faces pale, their throats choked with sobs, a strange peace flooded the grieving mother's heart.

"The Blessed Virgin was here when Francisco died!" she burst out suddenly. "I'm sure of it!"

Manuel Marto was sure of it, too, and for a long moment stood looking down at his wife, at the still figure of his little son. Then he pulled a rosary from his pocket and slowly got to his knees. Tears were streaming down his cheeks also, tears which he made no effort to hide.

"May God have mercy on the lad!" he sobbed. "And may He spare us our little Jacinta for a long time yet..."

Alas for the father's heartfelt prayer! As the April days succeeded one another and spring flowers studded the many new graves in Fatima's churchyard, Jacinta's health gave cause for real alarm. Like Francisco, she had been stricken with influenza around Christmas time. Slowly she had recovered, but only to be attacked by a new ailment. In her weakened condition she had fallen victim to a severe form of pleurisy. An abscess had formed in her side, and now there were many days when every breath was like a sharp swordthrust.

"Before very long I'll be in heaven with Francisco," the little girl confided to Lucia one afternoon when the latter had returned from a hard and lonely day at school. "Then your work will begin."

"*My* work?"

"Yes. Oh, surely you haven't forgotten! Why, you're to make people understand that Our Lord wants to establish in the world the devotion to the Immaculate Heart of Mary!"

Lucia shifted uncomfortably. "That's right. The lady did tell me that."

"Yes. And listen. You mustn't run away any more when people come and ask you questions. Tell everyone that God grants graces through the Immaculate Heart of Mary and that they mustn't be shy about asking her for them."

"But *strangers*, Jacinta! You know how they've always bothered us! Why, Francisco often hid under the bed when they came asking for him!"

At this, a strangely wise look crept into the eyes of the nine-year-old girl, a look which was made possible by the floods of heavenly grace filling her soul. "Don't you know that our comfort doesn't matter?" she asked. "What does matter is that Our Lord wants to have His Heart and the Immaculate Heart of His Mother honored together. Your work is to tell people this."

Lucia nodded soberly, recalling what the lady had said on her second visit in the Cova. "I suppose you're right. And when people want to know how to stop the war . . . "

"You're to tell them to ask for this favor in the name of the Immaculate Heart of Mary. After all, Our Lord has placed the peace of the world in her keeping."

Lucia's eyes glowed with reverent wonder as she regarded her little cousin. "How I wish that you could stay here and help me with these messages!" she exclaimed fervently. "Oh, Jacinta! I'm going to be so lonely when you leave me for heaven . . . "

The latter nodded with an understanding far beyond her years. "Yes. But you'll offer your loneliness for sinners and that way many of them will be saved. Oh, Lucia! Surely there's no better work than this—helping to keep men and women out of that terrible place!"

As always, there was real conviction in the little girl's voice when she spoke of hell. Never had she forgotten the dreadful vision which she and her companions had been granted on the occasion of the lady's third visit. Now, two years later, she could still tremble at the mere thought of it. Indeed, when she was strong enough to talk, she frequently chose hell as a topic of conversation between Lucia and herself.

"The people in hell—don't they ever come out, Lucia?"

"No."

"Not even after many, many years?"

"No. Hell never comes to an end."

"DON'T THE PEOPLE IN HELL EVER COME OUT?"

"And it's the same in heaven? Those who go to heaven really stay there always?"

"That's right. Heaven and hell are eternal. They never end."

"But don't the souls burning in hell turn to ashes? Don't they stop suffering some time?"

"No. They suffer forever and ever."

"If we pray very hard for the people in hell, will Our Lord let them come out?"

"No. The souls in hell never come out. Nor the souls in heaven. They stay where they are for all eternity."

These truths were so overpowering that Jacinta could scarcely bear to consider them! *Eternity!* How impossible it was to grasp! And to think that she, or any other person living in the world, could help to decide whether people would be happy in it forever or would go to hell to suffer the torments of the damned!

"Because it's true that even children can help sinners win the grace to go to heaven by praying and suffering for them," she told herself. "Or we can leave them alone and not bother about what happens. But how unkind that would be . . . and how terrible for the poor sinners and their families . . ."

Ever since the lady's third visit, Jacinta had grown in the grace of loving souls. Thus, she gladly wore the piece of rough rope about her waist, went without her lunch on many days, refrained from drinking cold water—offering up the suffering in satisfaction for the sins of those too lazy or careless to do penance for themselves. And she encouraged Francisco and Lucia to do the same. But when the influenza struck in December, 1918, such mortifications had to cease. Now that she was ill, it was no longer right to deprive herself of food and water. As for the rope about her waist . . .

"Take it and hide it for me," she told Lucia. "I don't want Mother to see it. If I get better you can give it back to me."

The older girl nodded. She had already performed a similar service for Francisco. But soon after his death she realized that neither would Jacinta ever wear the painful rope again. The pleurisy which had attacked her following the influenza was steadily growing worse.

"Oh, I wish you didn't have to suffer this way!" she cried one May day when she was permitted to visit briefly with her beloved cousin. "Jacinta, isn't there anything I can do to help?"

Gasping painfully for breath, the little patient shook her head. "No. And don't worry about me. I've ... I've had some wonderful news."

"What?"

"I'm going to make my First Communion!"

"No!"

"Yes. And now that Our Lord is coming, nothing matters, Lucia. Not anything!"

"But the suffering must be so terrible ... "

"Yes. But it's for souls, remember. And I'm sure it's helping someone, somewhere ... "

Undoubtedly God's mercy was allowing the merits of Jacinta's heroic charity to be applied to sinners, in Portugal and elsewhere. Certainly the names of Jacinta Marto and Lucia dos Santos were now famous throughout the country, and crowds flocked to the homes of the two little girls, to Francisco's humble grave, eager for favors and prayers. By now the little chapel in the Cova which the lady had asked to have erected in her honor was completed, and every day—on their way to and from the Marto and dos Santos houses—pilgrims were to be seen there offering five or more decades of the Rosary. Nor were these pilgrims always from far-away places. Many were residents of Fatima and the neighboring countryside, for no longer was there anyone in the district who scoffed at the apparitions in the sheep pasture. Indeed, in every home for miles around the Rosary was now offered with true devotion as the regular family prayer.

"It was really the Blessed Virgin who appeared to the children," the countryfolk agreed. "She told them to tell us to say the Rosary every day, and properly, so that she can give us many blessings. Well, we need these blessings. And of course we don't want to disobey the Mother of God."

How happy Jacinta was when she heard that friends and neighbors were learning to know and love the Rosary as never before! That because of this wonderful prayer, the spiritual tone of the whole village of Fatima had been raised and strengthened! And how her heart rejoiced when she discovered that friends and neighbors also said the prayer which the lady had taught on the occasion of her second visit—the prayer which was to follow the *Gloria* at the end of each mystery of the Rosary:

"*O Jesus, forgive us our sins! Save us from the fires of hell. Bring all souls to heaven, especially those who have most need of Your mercy!*"

"People are saying some of our other prayers, too," Lucia announced on the day following Jacinta's First Communion. "I've heard them."

Her heart still overflowing with the happiness of Our Lord's recent visit, Jacinta looked up eagerly. "Which prayers?"

" '*My God, I love You because of the graces which You have given me.*' "

"Yes, and what else do they say?"

116

" *'Sweet Heart of Mary, be my salvation.'* "

"And the offering before making a sacrifice for sinners—do they know that, too?"

"Yes. And they include the Holy Father now, just as we do."

"Oh, I love that prayer!" whispered Jacinta, her eyes shining. "It has so much in it. Let's say it together, shall we?"

So the two little cousins began to utter the familiar words which the lady had taught them so long ago: *"Oh, my Jesus, I offer this for the love of Thee, for the conversion of sinners, for the Holy Father and in reparation for all the wrongs done to the Immaculate Heart of Mary."*

Poor Jacinta! As the days passed, there were many occasions to make this offering. But a month after her First Communion there arrived an opportunity for suffering that really surpassed all the others. Then it was that Manuel and Olimpia Marto decided that their little girl should leave Fatima and go to Saint Augustine's Hospital in Ourem. There was a chance that regular medical treatments would cure the painful abscess in her side.

Dedicated though she was to suffering for sinners, nine-year-old Jacinta could hardly bear to think on the ordeal awaiting her. To go to Ourem, the town where she and her two playmates had once spent five terrible days in prison—this could never be a pleasant experience. But to go to the *hospital* there . . .

"When the lady visited Francisco and me, she said that I'd die in a hospital," the little one faltered when Lucia came to see her on her way home from school. "And she said I'd die alone. Oh, I can hardly bear *that!*"

"But the lady's coming to take you to heaven!" the older girl hastened to remind her, with a cheerfulness she did not really feel. "Surely this'll make up for everything! And just think! In heaven you'll see Francisco again!"

Face to face with the great sacrifice of saying good-bye to her best friend, Jacinta twisted uneasily. "Yes, of course. But if you could only come with me to Ourem! If you could only be with me when I die ... "

Lucia shook her head. "I guess that can't be," she muttered, and suddenly blinding tears sprang to her eyes. Jacinta was suffering terribly, of course. And it would be very hard for her to have to die alone in the hospital. But what of Lucia herself? When Jacinta was reunited with Francisco in heaven and the joys of Paradise were hers to enjoy forever, Lucia would still be suffering on earth. She would be quite alone then, for with Jacinta gone there would be no one in the whole world with whom she could talk freely about the lady, the various visions, the work she had been given to do in spreading devotion to the Immaculate Heart of Mary.

Slowly she knelt down beside her little cousin's bed. "I think we'd better say the prayer again," she whispered. "This is such a great sacrifice ... "

Chapter 14 — To Lisbon

IN ACCORDANCE with her parents' wishes, Jacinta spent the months of July and August at the hospital in Ourem. It was there that she received the distressing news that her uncle, Antonio dos Santos, the father of Lucia, had fallen ill of influenza and had died. But even as she sympathized with Lucia on the two occasions when the latter came to Ourem to visit her, Jacinta insisted that soon her own turn to go to heaven would come. She had suffered longer than either her brother or uncle. Why, it was midsummer now, and she had been ill since the previous Christmas!

But God did not will that the little girl should end her work of saving souls just yet. One day the doctors announced that she might as well return to Fatima. The two months of special treatments in Saint Augustine's Hospital had not done her the least good.

"I guess the lady's changed her mind," murmured the child when the news was brought to her. "Oh, and I'm glad! It will be much easier to die at home than in a hospital . . ."

But as autumn came to Fatima, Jacinta still lingered on—suffering and praying. As often as possible Lucia came to see her, bringing what wild flowers she could find in the fields. Then the little sufferer's eyes would brighten as she gazed on the colorful petals.

"You picked these daisies in the Cova, didn't you?"

"Yes."

"And the lilies at Valinhos?"

"That's right."

"Oh, Lucia, how good you are to me! And how I wish that I could go with you to pick the flowers! But tell me—do you pray for me at the new little chapel in the Cova—the one dedicated to Our Lady of the Rosary?"

"Of course. And I pray for you every day in the church in the village, too."

"What do you say for me to Our Lord?"

"What you told me to say: that you love Him very much. That you love Our Lady, too, and that you want to save as many souls as you can by suffering for their sins."

"That's nice. But Lucia—wouldn't it be fine if the lady could come again and we could tell her all these things in person?"

The latter nodded eagerly. "Oh, yes! That would be wonderful. But I guess she can't come to see us too often."

One day after Jacinta's return from Ourem, however, and without the slightest warning, the invalid's wish was granted. Yes, late in the year 1919, when no one was about in the Marto house, Our Lady of the Rosary appeared in all her shining beauty to her little friend.

OUR LADY OF THE ROSARY APPEARED TO JACINTA.

"Did she say that you'd be cured?" asked Lucia hopefully when Jacinta told her of Our Lady's visit.

The child shook her head. "No. She didn't tell me that."

"What did she say then?"

In spite of herself, the little girl's eyes filled with tears as she recalled the latest message from heaven. "She said that I'm going to go to another hospital, in Lisbon; that I'll suffer a great deal there and then die all alone ... "

"Oh, no, Jacinta! She didn't tell you *that!*"

"Yes. And then she said that I'll never see you again once I leave Fatima ... or any of my family ... and that even Mother will have to leave me in Lisbon ... "

The older girl could scarcely believe such sorrowful words. "Didn't the lady say anything nice?" she faltered.

"She told me not to be afraid, because in the end she herself will come and take me to heaven."

"But that's what she told Francisco just a few days before he died!"

"I know."

For a long moment the two looked at each other, hearts torn with grief. Then Lucia stretched out a comforting hand. "Don't think any more about it," she whispered.

At once the little sufferer's eyes lit up with a rare glow. "But I *want* to think about it! Don't you see that the more I think about what the lady said—about having to leave you and dying all alone in Lisbon—the more I suffer? And while there's time, I want to suffer all I can for the love of Our Lord and for souls!"

So the days passed, and in the middle of January, 1920, a celebrated eye specialist came on a pilgrimage to the Cova. He and his party called upon the dos Santos and Marto families, as did so many of the pilgrims. But the good doctor was less concerned with asking Jacinta questions about the heavenly lady than he was in helping her to feel better. Why, the poor little girl could scarcely breathe! And she was in such pain!

"You ought to arrange for the child to come to Lisbon," he urged the parents. "I'm sure that a friend of mine could perform an operation that would cure her completely. And you wouldn't have to worry about expenses. Other friends of mine would see to that."

Manuel and Olimpia Marto looked at each other doubtfully. Somehow, after so many months of sickness, they had come to feel that there was no hope for their little one. And yet how wonderful if in the great city of Lisbon, with its fine hospitals and clever surgeons . . .

"You owe it to Jacinta at least to try my plan," urged the eye specialist. Then, with a cheerful smile for the little invalid: "Wouldn't you like a trip to the city, my dear?"

Jacinta's eyes were full of tears. Slowly, surely, the events foretold by the lady on her latest visit were coming true. Here, for instance, was the beginning of the journey to Lisbon . . . the entrance into a second hospital . . .

"No, no!" she exclaimed weakly. "It would be just a waste of time to go there. And what's the use of an operation? After all, I'm never going to be well again . . . "

Such protests were in vain, however, and a few days later Jacinta and her mother set out for Lisbon. As she gazed at the familiar countryside, the little girl's heart was wellnigh breaking. Never again would she see these hills, these trees, these flocks of sheep grazing in the fields! As for her family, but more especially Lucia—oh, surely many sinners would be saved because of the sacrifice she had just made in saying good-bye to them!

"Don't worry, dear," Olimpia hastened to reassure her tenderly. "Our Lady is very good. I'm sure she'll cure you if we keep on asking her for the favor."

Jacinta smiled wanly. Her mother was so understanding! And she loved her so much! But to tell her for still another time that this farewell to Fatima was really a lasting one? Oh, no! Only to Lucia could she really unburden herself of such great suffering. And Lucia—ah, she would never see her again!

In due course the two travelers arrived in the capital. Arrangements had long ago been made for Jacinta to undergo a series of treatments before entering the hospital. While she was having these treatments, she was to stay with a certain family. But when these people laid eyes on the little invalid and noted her extreme frailty, they could not bring themselves to accept the responsibility of her care. So Olimpia had recourse instead to an institution, the Orphanage of Our Lady of Miracles.

This orphanage, which housed some twenty other children, was under the direction of Sister Mary of the Purification. But even though the latter was a nun, she did not wear a religious habit. Because of persecutions of the Church in Portugal, all convents and seminaries had been closed for several years, and those who had consecrated themselves by vow to God's service were required to wear secular dress. However, the religious spirit was still evident in such places as the orphanage, and though the children referred to Sister Mary of the Purification as "godmother," they all realized that she was a soul completely given to God and they loved and reverenced her accordingly.

Jacinta, suffering severely from the abscess in her side, was still able to walk about, and her heart filled with joy when Sister Mary of the Purification decided that she might pay an occasional visit to Our Lord in the Blessed Sacrament. Thus, whenever possible, the little girl went to a room which was attached to the chapel and from which she could look down into the sanctuary without being observed. Here she would stay for as long as was permitted, gazing longingly and lovingly at the Tabernacle. Such a privilege had been denied her for over a year—ever since she had fallen ill of the influenza—and now how much she appreciated it! And how she appreciated also the privilege of receiving Holy Communion frequently! Why, this was truly heaven on earth ...

Naturally Sister Mary of the Purification was much impressed with the little newcomer's piety. Then presently she was even more than impressed. She was dumbfounded! For one day as she entered Jacinta's room for a visit with her, the child started up anxiously from her pillow and shook her head.

"Would you mind coming back later, godmother? Right now I'm expecting the Blessed Virgin."

The Blessed Virgin! When the opportunity arose, Sister Mary of the Purification carefully questioned the little patient on this point, only to discover that since her arrival at the orphanage Jacinta had had several visions of Our Lady. The latter had comforted her when the pain was especially severe. She had also talked to her at considerable length on sin, war, the priesthood—subjects in which a little girl not yet ten years of age would scarcely be interested of herself.

"And what did Our Lady tell you about war?" asked Sister Mary, not quite ready to believe that Jacinta actually had been granted the great grace of seeing and speaking to the Mother of God. "Why do we have such a terrible thing as this in the world?"

Jacinta's eyes were grave. "The Blessed Virgin said that wars are nothing more than punishments for the sins of the world. And she said that she can no longer restrain the hand of her Son from striking the world. People must do penance. If they will do penance, Our Lord will pardon their faults once more. But if they do not change their lives, the punishment will come ... "

The good religious could scarcely believe her ears. That a child should speak with such precision on a matter far beyond her age and experience! And that she should also hint of another war to be visited upon the world, unless people changed their lives and did penance ...

"Now suppose you tell me what the Blessed Mother said about sin," she said gently.

For a moment Jacinta was silent, entering into herself as it were in order to recall Our Lady's words. Then she began to speak:

"The sins which cause most people to go to hell are the sins against purity."

"But child, do you know what it means to be pure?"

"Oh, yes. To be pure in body means to preserve one's chastity. To be pure in spirit means not to commit any sin, not to look at what does not concern one, not to steal, not to lie, always to tell the truth, no matter what it costs."

"And who taught you all these things?"

"The Blessed Virgin, godmother. Although some of them I found out by myself. You see, I love to think ... "

Sister Mary controlled her amazement as well as she could. "And what did Our Lady say about the priesthood?" she asked in a matter-of-fact voice.

Jacinta's eyes glowed. "She said that priests must be pure, very pure. They should not busy themselves with anything except what concerns the Church and souls. The disobedience of priests to their superiors and to the Holy Father is very displeasing to Our Lord."

"And what else, child?"

"We must pray for the governments of the world, godmother. If the government of a country leaves the Church in peace and gives liberty to our holy religion, it will be blessed by God."

Sister Mary of the Purification did not wish that Jacinta should tire herself with too much talking, but from time to time she had other inspiring conversations with the little girl. Then she learned that the Blessed Mother had told her that the approaching operation would be a failure. Also, that in a short time Florida and Therese Marto, her two sisters, would die.

"As for me, please let me be buried in my First Communion dress with the blue sash," the little one begged. "Blue and white are really Our Lady's colors, you know."

Sister Mary promised, hoping against hope that Jacinta was mistaken in the prophecy concerning her own welfare. After all, Doctor Leonardo de Castro Freire, one of the finest surgeons in Lisbon, was to perform the operation.

Alas for such hopes! Jacinta left the Orphanage of Our Lady of Miracles after two weeks and entered Saint Stephen's Hospital on February 2. Eight days later she underwent the operation, seemingly with good results. But soon her sufferings began again, and with even more intensity. Two ribs had been removed from the abscessed side, and the wound was causing terrible anguish. But the child was stirred almost into forgetting her dreadful sufferings when she heard certain of the doctors and nurses say that they did not believe in God.

"Poor unfortunate ones!" she would murmur sorrowfully. "They don't know what is waiting for them. Oh, if they could only understand something of the mystery of eternity! How they would do everything then to change their lives..."

From day to day Jacinta grew steadily weaker. Sister Mary of the Purification came to see her regularly and consoled her in her sufferings, which were now truly intense. Then one day she found her little friend resting easily.

"Why, I do believe you're better, Jacinta!" she cried joyfully. "How splendid!"

The child smiled. "No, godmother. But listen. Now I'm not complaining any more. The Blessed Virgin has appeared to me again. She promised to come for me soon, and she's taken away all my suffering. I no longer have the slightest pain."

Awestruck, Sister Mary drew closer to the bed. But Jacinta made a sudden motion with her hand. "Please don't stand there, godmother. That's where Our Lady stood. Come over here."

Promptly the latter obeyed, and soon Jacinta was describing the latest vision of the Queen of Heaven. Yes, Our Lady had appeared once more. But this time she had been sad—oh, so very sad!

"That's because many, many souls are going to hell on account of sins of impurity, godmother. Oh, people must turn away from their easy way of life and not give themselves up to sin as they have been doing! And it's absolutely necessary that they do great penance ... "

"Our Lady seemed very sad when she told you these things?"

"Oh, yes! Very sad! I felt so sorry for her ... "

Sister Mary was silent for a moment. Then she bent closer to the bed. "Jacinta, wouldn't you like to see your mother?"

The little one hesitated. Then, evading the question, she began to speak in a far-away voice. "My family will not stay on earth very long. Soon we shall all be together in heaven." And as her godmother stared incredulously, she gave a little sigh. "Our Lady told me that she will appear again, but not to me. Certainly I shall have died before then."

On February 20, ten days after her operation, Jacinta asked to receive the Sacraments. It was a Friday, and about six o'clock in the evening. Around eight o'clock a priest from the neighboring parish of the Holy Angels came to see the little patient. He heard her Confession but did not see fit to give her Holy Communion.

"Why, you're not in danger of death, child," he said cheerfully. "You look really well this evening."

At these words the little girl's eyes filled with tears. Here truly was the last great sacrifice to offer for sinners. For she *was* going to die, and in about two hours. Only recently Our Lady had told her the day and hour of her death. Now what sorrow not to be able to make the good priest understand ... and as a result, not to receive Our Lord in Holy Communion for just one more time ...

Chapter 15 Farewell to Fatima

OUR LADY of the Rosary came for Jacinta as she had promised at half-past ten that night. The child was a few days short of her tenth birthday. The last words to fall from her lips concerned those in charge of souls.

"Pray for the priests," she murmured. Then with a smile she entered upon eternity.

Back in Fatima, Lucia heard the news of her little cousin's passing with a breaking heart. Truly Jacinta had made no mistake when she had said that she would die in Lisbon, and that no operation, even by the most skilled surgeon, could save her.

"Now I'll never have anyone to talk to again!" the little girl told herself forlornly, tears streaming down her face. "First Francisco, then Jacinta! Oh, dear Blessed Mother, how hard it is to be alone!"

Soon Lucia was sadder than she had ever been in her whole life. Even the consolation of being able to pay frequent visits to Jacinta's grave was denied her, for the Baron d'Alvayazère, a devout nobleman, had asked for the privilege of keeping Jacinta's mortal remains in his family vault at Ourem. He felt that the body of a little girl who had seen the Blessed Virgin was a real treasure, and that great graces would be showered upon his family if he were allowed to honor it. And because of his high position and evident sincerity, his request had been granted. Jacinta's body had come by train from Lisbon to Ourem, then had been buried in the Baron's family vault.

Soon another great trial was visited upon Lucia. Following Jacinta's death on February 20, the atheistic government of Portugal increased its efforts to have the Cova da Iria closed as a place of devotion. The authorities had looked on with anxious displeasure when public subscription had built a little chapel there and dedicated it to Our Lady of the Rosary. They considered that it was bad enough for people still to go to church in village or town for Mass and the Sacraments, but that they should make difficult pilgrimages to such an out-of-the-way spot as Fatima—and in great numbers—was alarming. It showed that religion was far from being stamped out and that thousands of Portuguese men and women really believed in the existence of God.

As May 13, 1920, approached, the entire government grew uneasy. Somehow they felt that on this day—the third anniversary of the lady's first appearance in the Cova—a great pilgrimage to Fatima would suddenly take place. As in the past, there would be prayers, hymns and thousands of recitations of the Rosary. Perhaps there might even be some hysterical women to claim that they had been cured of this or that ailment by the Blessed Virgin. Then what outbursts of religious fervor! What extra rounds of Rosaries and other prayers!

"Why not call out the army to stop these stupid goings-on?" suggested one official grimly. "With armed guards on every road to Fatima, all instructed to arrest anyone found praying in the Cova, there certainly could be very little of a celebration."

No sooner said than done. For though Our Lady of the Rosary had proclaimed her identity on October 13, 1917, and had worked the great miracle she had promised, gradually the Devil had insinuated into the minds of his co-workers on earth the confidence to reject these events as superstitions. So it was that soon Lucia found herself suffering from still another cause than the loneliness which had fallen upon her with Jacinta's death three months earlier. After all, what could be more discouraging than to find that there were still unbelievers in the government—and this after the many prayers and sacrifices offered for them by Francisco, Jacinta and herself! That there were still those in Portugal who did not love Our Lady, who scoffed at prayer of all kinds, but particularly at the prayer of the Rosary!

"No matter what happens, I'll go to the Cova on the thirteenth," the child decided grimly. "If the soldiers kill me, so much the better. I'll offer myself for their sins, and then Our Lady will come and take me to heaven as she did Francisco and Jacinta."

Realizing something of what was taking place in her daughter's mind, Maria Rosa was worried. For a long time now she had realized that Lucia had never told a lie when she had said that she had seen and spoken with Our Lady. The great miracle of the "dancing sun" as well as the various cures worked in the Cova had convinced her that the little girl and her cousins really had been chosen by God to do some special work for souls. But it was disturbing to Maria Rosa to note the many hardships visited upon her dear ones since the first heavenly apparition. For instance, her nephew Francisco had died on April 4, 1919. Then her husband had followed on July 31 of the same year. After that her niece Jacinta had gone to God—on February 20, 1920. Now Jacinta's two sisters, Florida and Therese, were ailing, and it seemed unlikely that they would live for more than a few months. As for Olimpia Marto, her sister-in-law and the mother of Francisco, Jacinta, Florida and Therese, why, she was not at all well.

"Surely it can't be true what some people are saying," thought the good woman anxiously, "that all of us are going to die before our time as the price of the apparitions. Oh, dear God, it was hard enough to lose my husband, but if my children have to go, too . . . "

Poor Maria Rosa! Her heart was truly heavy when she saw Lucia making ready to go to the Cova on May 13, 1920. Like everyone else in Fatima, she had heard about the official declaration: that there was to be no public observance of this third anniversary of the lady's first visit; that even now a small army was being stationed in the Cova and along all roads leading to it with orders to see that no organized devotion should take place there.

"Child, don't go to pray in the Rosary Chapel today," she pleaded. "If the soldiers ever see *you*, they'll do something dreadful!"

Lucia scarcely seemed to hear the anxious words. "I'll be all right at Our Lady's shrine. And so will everyone else. Please don't worry, Mother."

Such confidence proved well-founded. Despite the soldiers, on the third anniversary of Our Lady's first visit to the little shepherds an immense pilgrimage was made to the Cova. True, all traffic had been stopped for miles about Fatima, but the thousands of pilgrims were not to be deterred by this. They had left their homes many hours ago to pay tribute to the Blessed Mother. Now, rather than return unsatisfied, they decided to abandon their wagons and bicycles, their oxen and mules, and proceed on foot to the sheep pasture. And to show what they thought of the atheists in Lisbon who had no love for Our Lady, they would sing hymns in her honor as they made their way through the fields.

Long before noon so many thousands of men and women had arrived at the sheep pasture that the soldiers were powerless to turn them away. And when the pilgrims began the recitation of the Rosary—their blended voices filling the Cova with wave upon wave of sound—all efforts to keep up an unfriendly front were abandoned.

"We believe in Our Lady of the Rosary just like everyone else," the soldiers finally admitted. "And it's not our fault that we had to try to stop the pilgrimage today."

"Then whose fault is it?"

"Why, the government's fault, of course."

"But didn't you intend to harm Lucia dos Santos?"

"*Harm Lucia?* Certainly not. Why, this child saw and spoke with the Blessed Virgin! We wouldn't touch a hair on her head!"

How relieved was Maria Rosa when she found that her youngest child was not to be hustled off to prison by the soldiers! Indeed, as the weeks passed and the monthly pilgrimages to the Cova continued, she experienced a certain satisfaction when she discovered that the vast crowds expected Lucia to lead them in the recitation of the Rosary. Yes, and she could even look upon the visits of José Alves Correia da Silva, Bishop of Leiria, without as much anxiety as formerly. After all, His Lordship was very kind and understanding. Whenever he came to Fatima (certainly the most famous spot in his whole diocese), he actually seemed to enjoy talking with poor countryfolk like herself.

Then one spring day in the year 1921 Maria Rosa was thrown into real confusion. The Bishop wished Lucia to leave Fatima! He thought she should become a student in a convent boarding school!

"The Sisters of Saint Dorothy have an excellent school at Vilar, near Porto, that would be the very place for Lucia," said His Lordship. "You see, the child's growing up and needs a better school than the one here in Fatima."

Not wishing to argue with the Bishop, Maria Rosa said nothing, although she could see no reason why Lucia needed any more schooling than she already had. Besides, how could she bear to have her youngest child leave home? The Bishop, however, understood what was taking place in the mother's heart and soon set her mind at ease by describing the fine school at Vilar, the holy Sisters who were so wise and clever and skilled in all branches of learning. Why, with them for teachers, Lucia would develop into a fine young woman! She would learn many more useful things than if she remained at home.

"Besides, I think it's no longer the best thing for our little one to be at the beck and call of so many hundreds of pilgrims here," concluded the Bishop. "She needs a change from Fatima, some peace and quiet. After all, she's been meeting strangers and answering their questions for four years. That's enough to try any child's strength to the limit."

"But the expense of sending her away to school, Your Lordship! Since my husband's death two years ago ..."

The Bishop smiled at Maria Rosa's anxious face. "Don't worry about the expense. I'll look after everything. The

main thing is that Lucia must have a chance to get more of an education than is to be had here. You see, God may have greater plans for her than anyone imagines. If so, and if she's to develop fully, she needs the proper training. Certainly the Sisters of Saint Dorothy can give her that. Why, they have the finest girls' schools in Portugal!"

So, even as Maria Rosa sought to readjust herself to this turn of events, the Bishop of Leiria began to make the necessary arrangements for Lucia to enter the boarding school conducted by the Dorotheans at Vilar. As for Lucia, she accepted the news in a manner not usual for a fourteen-year-old girl. She was neither pleased nor displeased. Somehow the various visits with Our Lady, the many prayers and sacrifices she had made for sinners during the past four years, had disposed her soul for the great grace of being completely abandoned to God's Will. Now it was sufficient that the Bishop wished her to go to Vilar. Nor would she question his decision that she was to enter the school not as Lucia dos Santos, the little girl who had seen and talked with the Blessed Virgin and was therefore famous throughout all Portugal, but as Maria das Dores, a nobody. If asked where she came from, she was not to mention Fatima. Rather, her home was to be "near Lisbon." And never, never was she to discuss Our Lady's visits with anyone. She was to be just a girl among other girls at the Sisters' boarding school.

"Promise that you'll remember all these things, Lucia," said the Bishop kindly. "Also, that you'll not tell anyone in Fatima about your going away."

Lucia nodded. "I give you my word, Your Lordship. And thank you so much for all your kindness. I know I'd never have been able to get a real education without your help."

As the warm spring days succeeded one another, it was decided that Lucia should leave for Vilar on June 21. True to her promise to the Bishop, she told no one of what was about to happen. Yet it was constantly in her thoughts, and on the afternoon before her departure Maria Rosa cast an anxious glance in her direction.

"You look pale, child. Why don't you take a walk in the fresh air?"

"But there's so much to do, Mother!"

"Nonsense. I can manage. You go for your walk. After all, it's your last day here."

A stab of pain shot through Lucia's heart at these words. *The last day here?* Oh, no! Surely this sacrifice wasn't to be required of her . . .

Yet as she made her way through the familiar fields, past the rows of olive trees that divided one neighbor's lands from another's, Lucia realized the truth: her mother had unwittingly spoken as a prophetess when she had said that this was Lucia's last day at home. Yes, Our Lady now wished that her little friend should say farewell to Fatima. Whatever work was in store for her was to be done elsewhere than in her birthplace.

The realization was so overwhelming that finally the fourteen-year-old girl could scarcely bear it. Tears in her eyes, she knelt upon the ground and let the soil slip through her fingers. This earth, this dry and porous limestone, had belonged to her family for generations. It . . . it was part of her! How could she leave it? How could she go to Vilar where she knew no one? Even more, how could she continue her walk today, gazing at the peaceful countryside for what her heart now told her was the last time?

"Oh, dear lady, please help me!" she sobbed. "I . . . I didn't know I wasn't coming back . . ."

The minutes passed, and finally a certain peace returned to the young girl's heart. And why? Because once again she had asked for and been given the grace to do not her will but the Will of God.

"I'll go on with my walk," she told herself. "No matter what it costs, I'll visit all the places I love."

There were many of these. The Cova, where Our Lady had appeared in all her shining beauty so many times; the parish church where Lucia had been baptized and had made her First Communion; the little cemetery adjoining, where Francisco and her own father lay buried; Valinhos, where Our Lady had paid her surprise-visit after the five-day imprisonment in Ourem; the various fields where Francisco and Jacinta had pastured their sheep; the cave where the Angel of Peace had shown himself and taught three little shepherds his beautiful prayers . . .

"Good-bye," whispered Lucia softly in each of these. "*Good-bye . . .*"

It was early the next morning, however, that the girl's heart was truly torn. At two o'clock, when the stars were like bright diamonds in the soft June sky, she arose from her bed, dressed, breakfasted, then went with her mother down to the road where her Uncle Manuel Correia was waiting with a donkey-cart to drive them to Leiria. Here they would meet a friend of the family who would take their young traveler to Vilar by train.

"We'll be passing the Cova, Lucia," said Uncle Manuel. "And we'll have time enough to stop in the chapel for a while. You'd like that, wouldn't you?"

The girl nodded. "Yes, Uncle. That would be very nice."

But she had not realized how hard it would be to keep back the tears as she knelt for the last time in the little chapel and recited five decades of the Rosary. It was so

"I DON'T WANT TO LEAVE!" SHE TOLD HERSELF.

peaceful here, with the rest of the world sunk in slumber. And what a soft radiance the little blue sanctuary lamp cast upon the plain plaster walls ... over the statue of Our Lady in the sanctuary ...

"I don't want to leave!" she told herself suddenly, torn with loneliness. "I ... I don't want to go to Vilar to be educated ... "

Maria Rosa and Uncle Manuel were quite unaware of what was running through her mind. "You may stay here a little while longer, Lucia," said her mother presently. "We'll drive down the road and wait for you there. But don't be too long, child. Remember, you have to catch a train in Leiria."

Lucia nodded. But when the door of the little chapel had shut behind her mother and uncle and their footsteps had faded away in the distance, she looked up at Our Lady's statue with eyes brimful of tears. Then slowly, forlornly, she uttered the words that were never far from her thoughts:

"Oh, my Jesus, I offer this for the love of Thee, for the conversion of sinners, for the Holy Father and in reparation for all the wrongs done to the Immaculate Heart of Mary."

As always, these words worked something of a miracle for the little girl. Her heart was still sad, but it was a holy sadness which she had experienced before—a sadness which she knew God wished her to endure for a little while for love of sinners. And as she gazed up through the blue-lit gloom at Our Lady's statue, it seemed that Francisco and Jacinta were suddenly close at hand. Long ago they had said farewell to Fatima. Oh, surely they were aware that now her turn had come ... that she was about to go away to school ... and that she needed their help and prayers ...

"Especially for the work that Our Lady said I must do," she whispered, "the work of spreading devotion to her Immaculate Heart. Oh, Francisco! Jacinta! How wonderful if some day not one but all three of us could help people to know and love the Immaculate Heart of Mary! And her Holy Rosary, too!"

And then it seemed as if familiar words were echoing through the shadows of the little chapel, words spoken by Jacinta in the last days of her life:

"Tell everybody that God gives graces through the Immaculate Heart of Mary. Tell them to ask these graces from her, and that the Heart of Jesus wishes to be venerated together with the Immaculate Heart of His Mother. Ask them to plead for peace from the Immaculate Heart of Mary, for the Lord has confided the peace of the world to her."

With sudden joy Lucia rose to her feet, the sadness completely gone now, her eyes shining. "Oh, I'll try to do it!" she whispered eagerly. "I'll try very hard ... "

St. Meinrad, Indiana
Feast of Our Lady of Mount Carmel
July 16, 1945

EDITOR'S NOTE: *Lucia remained as a student at Vilar for five years. Then on October 2, 1926, aged nineteen, she entered the Sisters of Saint Dorothy as a lay Sister. On October 3, 1928, she made her temporary vows, and on October 3, 1934, her perpetual vows. Upon entering religion, she was given the name of Sister Mary Lucia of the Dolors. She is still living today, at the Mother House of the Dorotheans in Tuy, Spain. According to reliable sources, Our Lady appears to her from time to time, encouraging her in the work of promoting devotion to the Immaculate Heart of Mary.*

From her convent home, Lucia recently made the following wonderful statement:

"I spend at Fatima every thirteenth day of each month in which the apparitions occurred. On the eve, during the Nocturnal Adoration, which I have not the permission to make in the chapel, my soul flies to Fatima and prostrates itself in the midst of the thousands of people kneeling before the Blessed Sacrament exposed. There I pray for everyone, and for myself, until my body here falls asleep...

"At dawn there is Mass in our convent chapel, at which I assist with my eyes closed. But it is in Fatima that I hear it in spirit, and there, too, do I receive Holy Communion in the open air, with the thousands of others. In the afternoon I say the Rosary here with my community, but really I am saying it with another group of people—the great crowds in the Cova da Iria. There, solitary in the midst of the pilgrims, I recall the first apparition. I see myself a child again, with Francisco and Jacinta. Once more I am walking upon the soil of the mountains, and I am seeing the young green oak trees which have not grown since I left them. Suddenly, a flash of lightning! What brilliance! What a sweet and heavenly voice! Ah, but how quickly everything passes away...the lady has gone...

"I hear the hymns of the great crowd pressing about me. I assist at the procession when Our Lady's statue is taken from the chapel, carried up the steps of the unfinished Basilica and held before the people, who wave their handkerchiefs in recognition of her. I assist at the Mass of the Sick. I ask Our Lord to have pity on all the sick, those sick in body as well as in soul. Then the Blessed Sacrament is carried by in procession, and I, in the midst of the sick people, cry out for a blessing. Finally everything is over. Before nightfall, I am back in the convent."

As this book goes to press (August, 1946) Sister Mary Lucia is thirty-nine years old.

Favorite Prayers of the Children of Fatima

I. *Between the decades of the Rosary, after the* Gloria:
Oh, Jesus, forgive us our sins! Save us from the
fires of hell. Bring all souls to heaven, especially
those who have most need of Your mercy.

II. *Ejaculations:*
My God, I love You because of the graces which
You have given me!
Oh, Jesus, I love You!
Sweet Heart of Mary, be my salvation!

III. *The offering before making a sacrifice:*
Oh, my Jesus, I offer this for the love of Thee, for
the conversion of sinners, for the Holy Father and
in reparation for all the wrongs done to the Immaculate Heart of Mary.

IV. *Prayers of the Angel of Peace:*
Oh, my God, I believe in Thee! I adore Thee! I
hope in Thee, and I love Thee! I ask pardon for
those who do not believe, do not adore, do not
hope, and who do not love Thee. (Three times)

Most Holy Trinity—Father, Son and Holy Ghost—
I adore You profoundly. I offer You the Most
Precious Body, Blood, Soul and Divinity of Jesus
Christ, present in all the tabernacles of the world,
in reparation for the insults, sacrileges and indifference whereby He is offended. By the infinite
merits of His Most Sacred Heart and of the Immaculate Heart of Mary, I beg of you the conversion
of sinners.

*N. B. Following the example of the Angel of Peace,
the children recited this last prayer kneeling, with
their foreheads touching the ground.*

Our Lady's Great Promise at Fatima

(June 13, 1917)

"My child, behold my heart surrounded with the thorns which ungrateful men place therein at every moment by their blasphemies and ingratitude. You, at least, try to console me. Make known to men that I promise to assist at the hour of death with the graces necessary for salvation, all those who, on the first Saturday of five consecutive months, shall

1. Go to Confession and receive Holy Communion,

2. Say the Rosary,

3. And spend a quarter of an hour with me in meditating on the fifteen mysteries of the Rosary,

4. With the object of making reparation to me."

N.B. The Confession may be made during the eight days before or after the Communion. The Rosary (five decades) may be recited at any convenient time of the day, and the fifteen minute meditation may be made at any time of the day, either on all the mysteries as a whole, or on one special mystery.

CPSIA information can be obtained at www.ICGtesting.com
Printed in the USA
LVOW10s1659110614

389607LV00015B/969/P